FIRST SETTLERS IN GEORGIA

VOLUME 6

Abstracts of English Crown Grants
in
St. John Parish, 1755–1775

BULLOCK, CANDLER, EVANS, LIBERTY,
LONG AND TATTNALL COUNTIES

Marion R. Hemperley
Surveyor General Department
State of Georgia

Heritage Books
2024

HERITAGE BOOKS

AN IMPRINT OF HERITAGE BOOKS, INC.

Books, CDs, and more—Worldwide

For our listing of thousands of titles see our website
at
www.HeritageBooks.com

A Facsimile Reprint
Published 2024 by
HERITAGE BOOKS, INC.
Publishing Division
5810 Ruatan Street
Berwyn Heights, MD 20740

Originally Printed 1972
by the State Printing Office
Atlanta, Georgia

Reprinted by Special Permission of
Georgia State Archives
1998

International Standard Book Number
Paperbound: 978-0-7884-2742-8

Introduction

The Royal Charter of June, 1732, given by King George II to the Trustees for Establishing the Colony of Georgia in America, defined the boundaries of the new colony as lying between the Savannah and Altamaha Rivers, extending as far north as those rivers flowed and thence from their sources in a straight line to the South Seas.

The land in question was in possession of the Creek and Cherokee Nations, and when James Edward Oglethorpe, one of the Trustees and the leader of the colony, landed at Yamacraw Bluff on the Savannah River on February 12, 1733, he was well aware that some agreement with the Indians was necessary. His first treaty with the Creeks in 1733 assured him of a small area along the Savannah River, running north along it to a point opposite today's Rincon, passing through that town and today's Eden in a diagonal line to the Ogeechee, thence south and a little west in a straight line to the Altamaha River, or, as it has been described elsewhere, "the area between the Savannah and the Altamaha as high as the tides flowed." This was the small part of the original charter grant in which the colonists settled and here they laid out the City of Savannah.

The 1733 Treaty with the Creeks reserved two parcels of land for themselves. One was an area from Pipemaker's Bluff to Palachucolas Creek and the other was the Islands of Ossabaw, Sapelo, and St. Catherine. It was not until 1757 at a congress held as Savannah that a treaty between the English and the Creeks gave to Georgia the three great Sea Islands and the small tract of land in reserve near Savannah. By this time, too, the colonists had settled considerably beyond the limits of the first treaty and came to look upon all this land as their own. Oglethorpe had early fortified St. Simons Island knowing well that it was outside of the treaty boundary as well as the charter limits. The next year in 1758, without treaty or permissions from the Indians, an Act of the Assembly created seven parishes, i.e., St. Paul, St. George, St. Matthew, Chrish Church, St. Philip, St. John and St. Andrew. By Royal Proclamation in 1763, the English Crown extended Georgia's southern boundary to the St. Marys River, and by Act of Assembly again, the four new parishes of St. David, St. Patrick, St. Thomas and St. Mary were created from that extension in 1765.

The Creeks were uneasy about these expansions and in order to quiet them and to redefine the western boundary, a new treaty

Introduction

was made in 1763 at Augusta. The limits of the settlers went as far as the Little River to the north, down the Ogeechee to the southwest corner of the present boundary line of Bulloch County, southward crossing the upper reaches of the Canoochee River and ended at the St. Marys.

The last of the Royal Provincial treaties was in 1773 and this included what was called the Ceded Lands, a rich area acquired from the Creeks and Cherokees north of the Little River to the Broad and west almost to the Oconee River. Settlement in this area was barely begun when the first fires of the Revolution were seen in the Province and until that war was over, Georgia remained a relatively narrow strip along the Savannah to the Ogeechee River.

Under the Trustees, from 1732 until the charter was resigned to the Crown in 1752, all allottments or leases of land made to the settlers were in Tail Male. Unlike fee simple grants, the leases could not be mortgaged, sold or otherwise disposed with. Some confusion exists about these allottments and leases, since some of the written records refer to them as grants, when, strictly speaking, that term is not correct. In 1752, after the relinquishment of the charter, Georgia became a Royal Province and under the English Crown and its Royal Governors, fee simple grants were made to the land which gave a clear title to the grantees. These Royal Grants, in the Georgia Surveyor General Department of the Office of the Secretary of State, begin in 1755. The three year gap between 1752 and 1755 is variously explained by historians, but in any case, the latter year is the first date for the grants. There are some 5000 of these recorded.

The department has now abstracted, very carefully and accurately, all of the Royal Provincial Grants. Using cards, citations to survey date, grant date, acres, name of grantee, page and book of record are shown, and a verbatim extraction of the description of the property granted. The legal verbiage of "Appurtenances and hereditaments" has been omitted. All else is shown in the abstract.

During the Revolution, according to one of the state's early Surveyors General, many of the plats of survey for the Royal Grants were destroyed. In abstracting the grants, it was found that only one grant in four had the plat of survey. Also, some plats existed for which there was no grant issued, although there were not many of these. In the text, where the reader

Introduction

finds no citation for a survey, there is none, and, conversely, where no grant is shown, there is none extant.

It is hoped that this effort will give important data to state officials first, and then to geographers, historians and the general public.

Addenda for St. John Parish

In order to make this work as complete as possible, the early
districts which preceeded the parishes will be included with
the parish grants. For St. John Parish this means the town of
Sunbury, St. Catherine and Bermuda Islands, District of Midway
and District of Newport, all of which became St. John Parish
in 1758.

The exact area covered by the districts of Provincial Georgia
has never been known and according to Dr. E. M. Coulter in
Wormsloe, (Athens, Georgia, 1955), page 97, "Previously the
various 'districts' had no clear limits but were vaguely described. . . ." From a study of the grants made in the districts
it was found that the land in Newport and Midway almost all
went into St. John Parish. The District of Newport was gen-
erally aroung the river of the same name, while the District
of Midway was likewise in the area of the Midway River.

According to Horatio Marbury and William H. Crawford in Digest
of the Laws of the State of Georgia, (Savannah, 1802), page
151, ". . .from Sunbury in the district of Midway and Newport
from the southern bounds of the parish of St. Philip, extending
southward as far as the north line of Samuel Hastings, and,
from thence southeast to the south branch of Newport, including
the islands of St. Katharine and Bermuda, and from the north
line of the said Samuel Hastings northwest, shall be and for-
ever continue a parish by the name of 'The parish of St. John
. . . .'" In other words this act, dated March 15, 1758,
designates the region between the Midway (known today as Med-
way) River and the South Newport River as St. John Parish.
This area forms present-day Liberty County.

Transition from Districts and Towns into
Parishes in 1758 and 1765 to Counties in 1777

1732 - 1758 Districts & Towns	1758 - 1765 Parishes	1765 - 1777 Parishes	1777 Counties
District of Augusta	St. Paul	St. Paul	Richmond
District of Halifax	St. George	St. George	Burke
District of Abercorn	St. Matthew	St. Matthew	Effingham
District of Goshen	St. Matthew	St. Matthew	Effingham
District of Ebenezer	St. Matthew	St. Matthew	Effingham
District of Ogechee (above Canoochee River)	St. Philip	St. Philip	Effingham
District of Ogechee (below Canoochee River)	St. Philip	St. Philip	Chatham
Town of Hardwick	St. Philip	St. Philip	Chatham
Town of Savannah	Christ Church	Christ Church	Chatham
District of Savannah	Christ Church	Christ Church	Chatham
Sea Islands north of Great Ogechee River	Christ Church	Christ Church	Chatham
Town of Sunbury	St. John	St. John	Liberty
District of Midway	St. John	St. John	Liberty
District of Newport	St. John	St. John	Liberty
St. Catherines Island	St. John	St. John	Liberty
Bermuda Island	St. John	St. John	Liberty
Town of Darien	St. Andrew	St. Andrew	Liberty
District of Darien	St. Andrew	St. Andrew	Liberty
Sapelo Island	St. Andrew	St. Andrew	Liberty
Eastwood Island	St. Andrew	St. Andrew	Liberty
Sea Islands between Great Ogechee & Altamaha Rivers	St. Andrew	St. Andrew	Liberty
Town of Frederica	St. James	St. James	Liberty
District of Frederica	St. James	St. James	Liberty
Great St. Simons Island	St. James	St. James	Liberty
Little St. Simons Island	St. James	St. James	Liberty
Sea Islands south of Altamaha River	St. James	St. James	Liberty
Between Altamaha & Turtle River		St. David	Glynn
Between Turtle and Little Satilla Rivers		St. Patrick	Glynn
Between Little Satilla & Great Satilla Rivers		St. Thomas	Camden
Between Great Satilla & St. Marys River		St. Mary	Camden

Horatio Marbury & William H. Crawford. Digest of the Laws of Georgia (Savannah 1802) P. 150-153.

State of Georgia. 1777 Constitution, Section 242.

Anderson, George

500 acres, St. John Parish

Granted January 7, 1772   Grant Book I, page 487

****

Andrew, Ann

450 acres, St. John Parish

Granted May 1, 1759   Grant Book B, page 94

Bounded on the north by Francis Arthur.

****

Andrew, Benjamin

500 acres, District of Newport

Granted October 31, 1755   Grant Book A, page 67

Bounded on the west by Richard Baker.

****

Andrew, Benjamin

200 acres, St. John Parish

Granted April 13, 1761   Grant Book C, page 401

Bounded on the west by William Baker, south by John Bacon and
Elizabeth Baker, east by John Humphreys.

****

Andrew, Benjamin

50 acres, St. John Parish

Granted June 2, 1767   Grant Book F, page 264

Bounded on the south by land granted the said Benjamin Andrew.

****

Andrew, Benjamin

400 acres, St. John Parish

Granted February 7, 1769   Grant Book G, page 262

Bounded on the west by Lydia Saunders, east by John Stevens.

****

Andrew, Benjamin

150 acres, St. John Parish

Granted April 3, 1770   Grant Book G, page 570

Bounded on the south by said Benjamin Andrew and vacant land, east by Grey Elliott.

****

Andrew, Benjamin

350 acres, St. John Parish

Granted February 5, 1771   Grant Book I, page 246

Bounded partly on the south by land of said grantee and partly by Joseph Andrew, on all other sides by vacant land.

****

Andrew, James

100 acres, St. John Parish

Granted April 1, 1759   Grant Book B, page 92

****

Andrew, James

350 acres, St. John Parish

Granted April 1, 1759   Grant Book B, page 93

Bounded on the east by Francis Arthur.

****

Andrew, Joseph

262 acres, St. John Parish

Granted March 1, 1763   Grant Book D, page 286

Bounded on the Southwest by salt marsh of Newport River and by part of the said river, west and northwest by John McGuire, north by William Low, southeast by John Lawson.

****

Andrew, Joseph

1000 acres, St. John Parish

Granted September 2, 1766   Grant Book E, page 349

Bounded on the southwest by John Davis.

****

Andrews, Benjamin

200 acres, District of Newport

Granted September 30, 1757   Grant Book A, page 569

Bounded on the southeast by William Clifton, south by William Graves, west by William Graves and John Stewart.

****

Antrobus, Isaac

20 acres, St. John Parish

Granted June 7, 1774   Grant Book H, page 105

Bounded on the north by a creek, east by Thomas Carr, west by John Lawson.

****

Arthur, Francis

344 acres, District of Midway, St. John Parish

Surveyed November 22, 1753   Plat Book C, page 1

Granted August 7, 1759   Grant Book C, page 205

Bounded on the east by marsh of a creek leading from the south side of Midway River, south by Edmund Tannatt, north by Middleton Evans. Surveyed as 350 acres (See Plat Book C, page 1).

****

Arthur, Francis

600 acres, St. John Parish

Granted August 7, 1759   Grant Book C, page 203

Bounded on the east by Phenney.

****

Arthur, Francis

100 acres, District of Midway, St. John Parish

Surveyed May 23, 1753   Plat Book C, page 4

Granted August 7, 1759   Grant Book C, page 207

Tract located on north side of Midway River, bounded on the west by Collins Creek, north by John Bennet.

****

Arthur, Francis

150 acres. south side of Midway River

Surveyed November 1, 1753   Plat Book C, page 1

No grant recorded.

Tract located on west side of Evans Creek on south side of Midway River. Bounded on the southeast by M. Rich. Harrard.

****

Arthur, Mary (wife of Francis Arthur)

200 acres, Bermuda Island, St. John Parish

Granted September 3, 1765   Grant Book E, page 222

Bermuda Island also known as Herrons Island. Originally ordered
Mary's late husband, John Stevens, deceased. Bounded on the west
by North Newport River and John Jones, north by Harriot Crook,
south by John Barnaby.

****

Ashmore, Strong

150 acres, St. John Parish

Granted October 4, 1774   Grant Book M, page 415

****

Bachelor, John

250 acres, St. John Parish

Granted June 7, 1774   Grant Book I, page 1029

Bounded on the west by land granted, northeast by James Butler.

****

Bacon, Joseph

500 acres, District of Midway

Granted March 5, 1756   Grant Book B, page 6

Bounded on the north by Sarah Mitchel, west by John Stewart, Sr.,
east by said Joseph Bacon.

****

Bacon, Joseph

500 acres, District of Newport

Granted March 5, 1756   Grant Book B, page 7

Bounded on the west by said Joseph Bacon, north by Sarah Mitchel,
east by Richard Spencer.

****

Bacon, Joseph

300 acres, District of Newport

Surveyed January 2, 1756   Plat Book M, page 35

Granted March 5, 1756   Grant Book B, page 8

Bounded on the east by Elizabeth Baker, south by Moses Way, west by William Baker.

****

Bacon, Joseph; Osgood, John; Stevens, John; Elliott, John; Baker, William; Way, Parmenus; Quarterman, John; Winn, John; Graves, John; Baker, Richard (all trustees)

300 acres, District of Midway

Granted September 8, 1756   Grant Book A, page 327

Bounded on the west by Nathaniel Way. Land granted in trust for the use of the minister for the time being of the Dissenting or Congregational Church erected or to be erected in the District of Midway and Newport.

****

Bacon, Samuel

500 acres, District of Midway

Granted May 15, 1756   Grant Book A, page 195

Bounded on the east by Kenneth Bailey.

****

Bacon, Samuel

300 acres, St. John Parish

Granted January 1, 1771   Grant Book I, page 233

Bounded on the southwest by land of the estate of Kenneth Baillie, northwest by Joseph Oswell, northeast by Benjamin Andrew, partly northeast and partly southeast by Joseph Stephens and partly by vacant land.

****

Bacon, William

71 acres, St. John Parish

Granted October 7, 1766   Grant Book E, page 377

Bounded on the northeast by Joseph Bacon, east by Benjamin Lewis, west by land surveyed for Thomas Peacock.

****

Bacon, William

76 acres, St. John Parish

Granted June 7, 1774   Grant Book H, page 102

Bounded on the northwest by William Jones and John Oswell, southwest by William Jones, southeast by Thomas Young, northeast by Joseph Clay.

****

Baillie, Alexander

100 acres of marsh, St. John Parish

Granted May 1, 1756   Grant Book B, page 83

Bounded on the southwest by lands formerly Robert Howarth, northeast by part of an island belonging to Kenneth Baillie, on all other sides by marshes of Midway River.

****

Baillie, Kenneth

500 acres, District of Midway

Granted June 7, 1757   Grant Book A, page 382

Bounded on the east by Kenneth Baillie, Jr., all other sides by the Midway River and marshes of same.

****

Baillie, Kenneth

350 acres, District of Midway

Granted February 5, 1757   Grant Book A, page 383

Bounded on the east by Thomas and William Carr and a northern branch of the North Newport River, southwest by Robert Baillie, northwest by Sanuel Burnley.

****

Baillie, Kenneth

500 acres, District of Midway

Granted June 7, 1757   Grant Book A, page 404

Bounded on the north by Audley Maxwell, Jr., east by marshes of Midway River.

****

Baillie, Kenneth

100 acres, St. John Parish

Granted May 1, 1759   Grant Book B, page 73

Tract is part of an island called Baillie's Island bounded on the west by Kenneth Baillie, Sr., and on all other sides by the Midway River and marshes of the same.

****

Baillie, Kenneth

200 acres, District of Midway, St. John Parish

Surveyed January 3, 1758   Plat Book C, page 32

Granted May 1, 1759   Grant Book B, page 82

Bounded on the north by said Kenneth Baillie, west by Robert Carr, east by Nathaniel Way. Surveyed as Kenneth Bailey.

****

Baillie, Robert

500 acres, District of Newport

Granted September 30, 1757   Grant Book A, page 459

Bounded on the west by Newport River.

                         ****

Baillie, Robert Carnibe

179 acres, St. John Parish

Granted June 7, 1774   Grant Book I, page 1045

Bounded on the north by Kenneth Baillie, east by Andrew Darling,
south by Parsonage land and land of Palmer Bolding, west by
lands of Palmer Golding. Tract is surplus land contained within
the lines of a tract surveyed for Kenneth Baillie, deceased.

                         ****

Baillou, James

200 acres, St. John Parish

Granted December 3, 1760   Grant Book B, page 497

Bounded on the east by Evan's Creek (a branch of Midway River)
and marshes thereof, south by Richard Hazard, west and north
by Edmund Tannatt.

                         ****

Baillou, John

300 acres on south side of Midway River

Surveyed March 18, 1748/9   Plat Book C, page 9

No grant recorded.

Originally surveyed for, and probably alloted to, John Baillou
and purchased from him by Peter Baillou. Bounded on the south
by Midway River, north and northeast by marsh.

                         ****

Baillou, Peter

300 acres on south side of Midway River

Surveyed March 18, 1748/9   Plat Book C, page 9

No grant recorded.

Originally surveyed for, and probably alloted to, John Baillou and purchased brom him by Peter Baillou. Bounded on the south by Midway River, north and northeast by marsh.

****

Baillou, Peter

300 acres on south side of Midway River

Surveyed March 18, 1748/9   Plat Book C, page 5

No grant recorded.

Originally surveyed for, and probably alloted to, Jonathan Calkins and purchased from him by Peter Baillou. Bounded on the north and northeast by marsh.

****

Baker, Benjamin

500 acres, District of Midway

Granted November 14, 1755   Grant Book A, page 70

Bounded on the east by Samuel Bacon, north by Andrew Collins.

****

Baker, Benjamin

200 acres, St. John Parish

Surveyed April 2, 1759   Plat Book C, page 21

Granted December 3, 1760   Grant Book C, page 316

Bounded on the west by William Baillou, north by Lewis Johnson, east by Abraham Frisby.

****

Baker, Benjamin

400 acres, St. John Parish

Surveyed March 23, 1761   Plat Book C, page 22

Granted July 5, 1774   Grant Book M, page 17

Bounded on the north by said Benjamin Baker, Ellis, and Phrisby, southwest by John Graves, southeast by John Quarterman.

****

Baker, Elizabeth

400 acres, District of Midway

Granted May 15, 1756   Grant Book A, page 215

Bounded on the east by Richard Baker.

****

Baker, James

250 acres, St. John Parish

Surveyed May 2, 1761   Plat Book C, page 20

No grant recorded.

Original warrant says land located at Newport. Bounded southwest by Nathaniel Clarck, west by James Mackay, north by John Stewart, east by Edward Way.

****

Baker, John

100 acres, District of Newport

Granted September 30, 1757   Grant Book B, page 15

Bounded on the north by Newport River, east by James Prichard, west by William Low.

****

Baker, John

50 acres, St. John Parish

Surveyed May 8, 1761   Plat Book C, page 20 and 31

Granted January 1, 1765   Grant Book E, page 99

Bounded on the east by Andrew Way and James Drickard, north
by John Baker, west by William Low, south by vacant land.

****

Baker, John

500 acres, St. John Parish

Granted December 2, 1766   Grant Book F, page 10

Bounded on the southeast by Francis Mitchell.

****

Baker, John

300 acres, St. John Parish

Granted June 2, 1772   Grant Book I, page 651

****

Baker, John

200 acres, St. John Parish

Granted July 5, 1774   Grant Book M, page 11

Bounded on the northeast by John Sullavan, southeast by John
Baker.

****

Baker, John

350 acres, St. John Parish

Granted January 3, 1775   Grant Book M, page 858

****

Baker, John Jr.

200 acres, St. John Parish

Granted July 5, 1774   Grant Book M, page 18

****

Baker, John Sr.

50 acres, St. John Parish

Granted April 3, 1764   Grant Book D, page 411

Bounded on the west by the said John Baker, north by John Mitchell, south by John Stewart, southeast by Joseph Gibbons.

****

Baker, Richard

500 acres, District of Midway

Granted October 31, 1755   Grant Book A, page 27

****

Baker, Richard

250 acres, St. John Parish

Original survey date unknown but resurveyed on March 31, 1818
Plat Book M, page 96

Granted July 1, 1760   Grant Book C, page 327

Tract found to contain 308 acres upon resurvey in 1818. Resurvey plat shows tract bounded on the north by Strong (land granted to Strong Ashmore), east by Thomas Chistee (granted to Ashmore), south by Benjamin Mell (granted to Richard Baker), west by estate of Thomas Bacon (granted to Ann Andrew).

****

Baker, Richard

100 acres, St. John Parish

Granted July 1, 1760   Grant Book C, page 329

Bounded on the north by said Richard Baker.

****

Baker, Richard

150 acres, St. John Parish

Granted December 7, 1762   Grant Book D, page 259

Bounded on the east by said Richard Baker, north by Ann Andrews, south by Benjamin Baker, Jr.

****

Baker, Richard

300 acres, St. John Parish

Granted August 2, 1774   Grant Book M, page 154

Bounded on the southeast by Josiah Powell.

****

Baker, Richard; Osgood, John; Stevens, John; Elliott, John; Baker, William; Bacon, Joseph; Way, Parmenus; Quarterman, John; Winn, John; Graves, John (all trustees)

300 acres, District of Midway

Granted September 8, 1756   Grant Book A, page 327

Bounded on the west by Nathaniel Way. Land granted in trust for the use of the minister for the time being of the Dissenting or Congregational Church erected or to be erected in the District of Midway and Newport.

****

Baker, William

500 acres, District of Midway

Granted January 16, 1756   Grant Book A, page 26

****

Baker, William

250 acres, District of Newport

Survey date not given   Plat Book M, page 34

Granted September 8, 1756   Grant Book A, page 194

Bounded on the west by Josiah Powell, east by Joseph Bacon.

****

Baker, William

100 acres, St. John Parish

Surveyed November 22, 1759   Plat Book M, page 33

Granted July 1, 1760   Grant Book B, page 419

Bounded on the south by said William Baker, east by Benjamin
Andrews (Plat shows bounded on the east by Benjamin Anderson,
not Andrews).

****

Baker, William

100 acres, St. John Parish

Granted July 1, 1760   Grant Book B, page 420

Bounded on the southwest by John Osgood and Joseph Way, east
by John Stewart, north by David Tobear.

****

Baker, William; Osgood, John; Stevens, John; Elliott, John;
Bacon, Joseph; Way, Parmenus; Quarterman, John; Winn, John;
Graves, John; Baker, Richard (all trustees)

300 acres, District of Midway

Granted September 8, 1756   Grant Book A, page 327

Bounded on the west by Nathaniel Way. Land granted in trust for
the use of the minister for the time being of the Dissenting or
Congregational Church erected or to be erected in the District
of Midway and Newport.

****

16

Baker, William Jr.

350 acres, St. John Parish

Granted November 2, 1762   Grant Book D, page 235

Bounded on the northeast by John Quarterman, northwest by Isaac Hauskins.

****

Baker, William Jr.

250 acres, St. John Parish

Granted May 1, 1770   Grant Book I, page 1

Bounded on the southeast by Samuel Jeans, southwest by John Baker, Jr.

****

Barber, John

111 acres, St. John Parish

Surveyed May 17, 1760   Plat Book C, page 22

Granted May 5, 1767   Grant Book F, page 219

The 111 acres being sundry small islands in the Sapelo River and bounded on every side by the marshes and creeks of the said river. Plat shows this tract including Richard Oldnors Island, John Barbers Island, and Warhue Island. Original warrant states that it is "sundry hammocks between South Newport and Sapelo Rivers at the head of Sapelo Sound."

****

Barnaby, John

250 acres, St. John Parish

Granted December 4, 1759   Grant Book B, page 345

Bounded on the north by vacant land, on every other side by marshes and creeks of Newport River.

****

Bateman, Mary (widow)

300 acres, District of Newport

Granted December 9, 1756   Grant Book A, page 351

Bounded on the east by Robert Smallwood.

****

Beard, Matthew

200 acres, St. John Parish

Granted August 2, 1774   Grant Book M, page 158

Bounded on the northeast by John Baker and vacant land, northwest by Mr. Butler.

****

Bosomworth, Adam

300 acres, District of Newport, St. John Parish

Granted May 1, 1759   Grant Book B, page 159

Bounded on the north by Newport River, east by Elizabeth De-
St. Julian, west by George Loves.

****

Bosomworth, Adam

500 acres, District of Newport, St. John Parish

Granted May 1, 1759   Grant Book B, page 160

Bounded on the north by Newport River, east by Burtley and
Daniel Mackay, south and west by said Adam Bosomworth.

****

Bosomworth, Mary

6200 acres, all of St. Catherines Island, St. John Parish

Granted June 30, 1760   Grant Book B, page 374

Bounded on the north by St. Catherines Sound, east by the ocean
and south by Sapelo Sound.

****

Bourquin, Henry Lewis

500 acres, St. John Parish

Granted October 6, 1772   Grant Book I, page 759

Bounded on the southeast by Charles Marines.

****

Bourquin, Henry Lewis

250 acres, St. John Parish

Granted October 6, 1772   Grant Book I, page 764

Bounded on the southeast by Henry Bourquin.

****

Brown, Francis

300 acres, St. John Parish

Granted February 5, 1765   Grant Book E, page 108

Bounded on the south by Alexander Ross and vacant land, west
by Raymond· Demere.

****

Brown, Francis

200 acres, St. John Parish

Granted May 2, 1769   Grant Book G, page 310

Bounded on the northwest by Francis Brown, east by John Quarterman and vacant land.

****

Brunson, Daniel

100 acres, St. John Parish

Granted September 6, 1774   Grant Book M, page 289

Bounded on the southeast by unknown.

****

Brunson, Daniel

100 acres, St. John Parish

Granted September 6, 1774   Grant Book M, page 290

****

Bryan, Jonathan

150 acres, St. John Parish

Surveyed February 17, 1761   Plat Book C, page 23

Granted August 3, 1762   Grant Book D, page 152

Tract located in the forks of the South and North Newport Rivers. Bounded on the northwest by land already granted to him, on every other side by salt marsh.

****

Bryan, Jonathan and Deveaux, James

400 acres, St. John Parish

Surveyed May 10, 1759   Plat Book C, page 21

Granted June 5, 1759   Grant Book B, page 153

Bounded on the north by Samuel Burnley and Phillippa Fenny, east by Josiah Powell.

****

Brydie, David

500 acres, St. John Parish

Granted November 6, 1770   Grant Book I, page 177

****

Brydie, David

150 acres, St. John Parish

Granted January 1, 1771   Grant Book I, page 234

Bounded on the northwest by land of the said grantee.

****

Burnet, John

150 acres, St. John Parish

Granted September 25, 1760   Grant Book C, page 312

Bounded on the north by William Johnson, east and west by vacant
land, on every other side by North Newport River and the marshes
thereof.

****

Burnet, John

57 acres, St. John Parish

Granted September 25, 1760   Grant Book C, page 314

Bounded on the northwest by Richard Burtly, southwest by Thomas
White, east by North Newport River, northeast and southeast
by marshes of North Newport River.

****

Burnley, Samuel

500 acres, District of Midway

Granted May 15, 1756   Grant Book A, page 113

Bounded on the southeast by Robert Ballie.

****

Burnley, Samuel

300 acres, District of Newport

Granted December 9, 1756   Grant Book A, page 359

Bounded on the east by Josiah Powell.

****

Burnley, Samuel

100 acres, St. John Parish

Surveyed October 4, 1759   Plat Book C, page 21

Granted May 21, 1762   Grant Book D, page 140

Bounded on the west by said Samuel Burnley.

****

Burrington, Thomas, as trustee for William Clifton

500 acres, District of Newport

Granted August 9, 1758   Grant Book B, page 2

Tract was known as Clifton and was originally granted William Clifton on March 5, 1756 (See Grant Book A, page 188) thence resigned on August 9, 1758 (See original order in Grant Book B, facing page 2). It was regranted on August 9, 1758 to **Thomas** Burrington as trustee for William Clifton and his heirs (See Grant Book B, page 2). Bounded on the south by a branch of Newport River, southeast (or east) by William Peacock, northeast by Josiah Osgood and Richard Spencer.

****

Burtley, Richard

300 acres, District of Newport, St. John Parish

Granted August 7, 1759   Grant Book B, page 137

Bounded on the west by Mr. St. Julian, south by Donald McKay, north by Newport River.

****

Burton, Robert

100 acres, St. John Parish

Granted July 1, 1760   Grant Book B, page 501

****

Butler, Elisha

500 acres, District of Newport

Granted September 30, 1757   Grant Book A, page 536

Bounded on the east by William Elliott, west by Thomas Way.

****

Butler, Elisha

300 acres, St. John Parish

Granted March 6, 1770   Grant Book G, page 534

Bounded on the southwest and southeast by said Elisha Butler, northeast by William Quarterman.

****

Butler, Joseph

460 acres, District of Newport

Granted December 6, 1757   Grant Book A, page 521

Bounded on the east by Charles West, southwest by John Mackintosh.

****

Butler, Joseph

750 acres, St. John Parish

Granted July 4, 1769   Grant Book G, page 350

****

Butler, Joseph

800 acres, St. John Parish

Granted August 1, 1769   Grant Book G, page 380

Bounded on the southeast and southwest by John Mitchell.

****

Butterfield, Francis

500 acres, St. John Parish

Granted January 4, 1763   Grant Book D, page 269

Tract situate and being on an island called Bermuda on the
south side of Midway River formerly alloted to Johannes Van
Beverhoudt whose right therein has been purchased by the said
Francis Butterfield. Bounded on the south by vacant land,
west by Col. Alexander Heron, deceased, east by creeks and
marshes of North Newport River and north by land of said Francis
Butterfield.

****

Butterfield, Francis

500 acres, St. John Parish

Granted January 4, 1763   Grant Book D, page 270

Tract situate and being on an island called Bermuda on the
south side of Midway River formerly alloted to Adrian Van
Beverhoudt whose right therein has been purchased by the said
Francis Butterfield. Bounded on the south by said Francis
Butterfield, west by land of the late Col. Alexander Heron,
deceased, on every other side by Midway River and the marshes
thereof.

****

Cain, John

200 acres, District of Midway

Granted March 28, 1758   Grant Book A, page 630

Bounded on the south by John Humphrey.

****

Calkins, Jonathan

300 acres, St. John Parish

Surveyed March 18, 1748/9   Plat Book C, page 5

Tract located on the south side of Midway River, originally
surveyed for and probably alloted to Jonathan Calkins and purchased
by Peter Baillou. Bounded on the north and northeast by marsh land.
****

Carney, Arthur

150 acres, St. John Parish

Granted December 3, 1761   Grant Book C, page 180

Bounded on the southwest by Moton Davis.

****

Carr, Mark

500 acres, District of Midway

Granted April 5, 1757   Grant Book A, page 429

Bounded on the east by Midway River, west by Thomas Carr, south by vacant land, all other sides by marshes of Midway River.

****

Carr, Mark

200 acres, District of Midway

Granted April 5, 1757   Grant Book A, page 430

Tract located between the Midway River and branches of St. Catherine River. Bounded by the said branches and large marshes.

****

Carr, Mark

500 acres, St. John Parish

Granted May 1, 1759   Grant Book B, page 71

Bounded on the north by William Carrs.

****

Carr, Mark

150 acres, St. John Parish

Granted May 7, 1765   Grant Book E, page 150

Tract "being the front of five hundred acres formerly granted to the said Mark Carr." Bounded on the west by said tract, east by Midway River.

****

Carr, Robert

100 acres, District of Midway

Surveyed March 3, 1757   Plat Book C, page 39

No grant recorded.

Bounded on the north by Capt. Kenneth Ballie, west by Samuel Bacon. Original warrant says tract located on South Branch, Midway River.

****

Carr, Thomas

500 acres, District of Midway

Granted April 5, 1757   Grant Book A, page 431

Bounded on the north by Midway River and marshes of same, east by Mark Carr.

****

Carr, William

500 acres, District of Midway

Granted February 7, 1758   Grant Book A, page 655

Bounded on the south by Mark Carr.

****

Carr, William

250 acres, St. John Parish

Surveyed May 3, 1760   Plat Book C, page 39

No grant recorded.

Original warrant says tract located on Demetres Neck, Newport River, bounded by John Burnet.

****

Carter, Thomas

200 acres, District of Newport

Granted May 15, 1756   Grant Book A, page 183

Bounded on the north by Newport River, west by said Thomas Carter, east by Clement Martin.

****

Carter, Thomas

300 acres, District of Newport

Granted September 8, 1756   Grant Book A, page 205

Tract known as Hepworth, bounded on the north by Newport River.

****

Carter, Thomas

100 acres, District of Newport

Granted April 5, 1757   Grant Book A, page 363

Bounded on the east by said Thomas Carter, west by Edward Mugguires, north by Newport River.

****

Carter, Thomas

150 acres, St. John Parish

Granted July 7, 1761   Grant Book D, page 13

Bounded on the north by said Thomas Carter, east by said Thomas Carter and John Elliott, southwest by Andrew Way.

****

Carter, Thomas

100 acres, St. John Parish

Granted October 6, 1772   Grant Book I, page 766

Bounded on the south by Lemon Munro, east by William Quarterman.

****

Carter, Thomas

300 acres, St. John Parish

Surveyed June 2, 1761   Plat Book C, page 39

Granted November 2, 1762   Grant Book D, page 223

Bounded on the northeast by William Baker, Jr., southwest by Isaac Hauskins. Tract surveyed as Thomas Carter and granted as Thomas Cater.

****

Cater, Stephen

415 acres, St. John Parish

Granted February 5, 1760   Grant Book B, page 357

Bounded on the east by Baillies Island, southwest by said Baillie, southeast by Nathaniel Way, west by Audley Maxwell, Jr., north by Audley Maxwell, Sr., northwest and southeast by a tract of 100 acres of marsh land granted Alexander Baillie.

****

Cater, Thomas

300 acres, St. John Parish

Surveyed June 2, 1761   Plat Book C, page 39

Granted November 2, 1762   Grant Book D, page 223

Bounded on the northeast by William Baker, Jr., southwest by Isaac Hauskins. Tract surveyed as Thomas Carter and granted as Thomas Cater.

****

Cater, Thomas

100 acres, St. John Parish

Granted April 5, 1763   Grant Book D, page 298

Bounded on the southeast by said Thomas Cater.

****

Clancey, Thomas

116 acres, St. John Parish

Granted December 4, 1759   Grant Book B, page 326

Bounded on the north by Hazard, on every other side by marshes of Midway and Newport Rivers.

****

Clark, Joshua

100 acres, St. John Parish

Surveyed October 11, 1759   Plat Book C, page 39

No grant recorded.

Bounded on the north by Thomas Magett. Original warrant says Magee and original plat says Maggee.

****

Clark, Stephen

150 acres, District of Midway

Surveyed December 7, 1757   Plat Book C, page 40

No grant recorded.

Original warrant says tract located at the head of the Middle
Branch, North Newport River south of land granted to Phillippa
Fenny.

****

Clifton, William

500 acres, District of Newport

Granted March 5, 1756   Grant Book A, page 188

Tract was known as Clifton and was originally granted William
Clifton on March 5, 1756 (See Grant Book A, page 188) thence
resigned on August 9, 1758 (See original order in Grant Book
B, facing page 2). It was regranted on August 9, 1758 to Thomas
Carrington as trustee for William Clifton and his heirs (See
Grant Book B, page 2). Bounded on the south by a branch of
Newport River, southeast (or east) by William Peacock, north-
east by Josiah Osgood and Richard Spencer.

****

Collins, Andrew

200 acres, District of Midway

Granted May 15, 1756   Grant Book A, page 209

Bounded on the north by Isaac Lines.

****

Cowper, Basil; Telfair, William; Telfair, Edward

1000 acres, St. John Parish

Granted June 5, 1770   Grant Book I, page 42

Bounded on the northeast by Henry Lewis and vacant land, southwest by John Collin and land heretofore laid out, on all other
sides by vacant land.

****

Crooke, Harriotte (widow)

500 acres on Bermuda Island

Granted February 7, 1758   Grant Book A, page 606

Tract located between the Newport and Midway Rivers bounded
on the east by Colonel Alexander Heron, south by vacant land,
all other sides by marshes and creeks of the Midway River.

****

Cubbage, John

300 acres, District of Midway, St. John Parish

Granted May 1, 1759   Grant Book B, page 105

Bounded on the east by Midway River, south by John Hancock and partly
by marshes and creeks.

****

Darling, Andrew

24 acres, St. John Parish

Granted April 3, 1770   Grant Book H, page 41

Bounded on the southeast by James Harley, northeast by Nathaniel
Way, west by the Glebe land.

****

Darling, Kenneth Baillie

125 acres, St. John Parish

Granted May 4, 1773   Grant Book I, page 970

Bounded on the north by Kenneth Baillie, east by Robert Carr,
south by Golding, west by Nathaniel Way and the Glebe land.

****

Davis, John

450 acres, District of Newport

Granted June 7, 1757   Grant Book A, page 409

Bounded on the east by Audley Maxwell.

****

Davis, John

500 acres, District of Midway

Granted June 7, 1757   Grant Book A, page 412

Bounded on the north and west by James and William Dunham,
east by James Maxwell, south by marshes of the Midway River.

****

Davis, John

100 acres, District of Midway, St. John Parish

Granted December 3, 1760   Grant Book C, page 184

Bounded on the north by said John Davis.

****

Davis, John

200 acres, District of Midway, St. John Parish

Granted December 3, 1760   Grant Book C, page 186

Bounded on the southwest by Parmenus Way, southeast by James
Maxwell.

****

Davis, John

400 acres, St. John Parish

Granted March 3, 1767   Grant Book F, page 106

****

Davis, John

300 acres, St. John Parish

Granted October 4, 1774   Grant Book M, page 428

Bounded on the south by John Davis, southwest by Captain John Winn, north by Benjamin Andrew.

****

Davis, John

500 acres, District of Midway

Surveyed September 14, 1752   Plat Book C, page 50

No grant recorded.

Tract known as Silk Grass Hill.

****

Davis, Scotton

200 acres, St. John Parish

Surveyed April 8, 1760   Plat Book C, page 52

No grant recorded.

Bounded on the northeast by Arthur Carney.

****

Davis, William

200 acres, District of Newport

Granted June 7, 1757   Grant Book A, page 413

Bounded on the north by a creek of the South Newport River, south by a marsh.

****

Dawson, William

100 acres, St. John Parish

Granted January 3, 1775   Grant Book M, page 868

Bounded on the north by Samuel Burley, southwest by Mr. Baillie, Mr. Thompson, and Mr. Nicholls.

****

Demere, Raymond

425 acres, St. John Parish

Granted December 7, 1762   Grant Book D, page 253

Bounded on the north by Clement Martin, south by Richard Hunt, west by William Graves.

****

Demetre, Daniel

500 acres, District of Newport

Surveyed May 10, 1750   Plat Book C, page 46

Granted May 15, 1756   Grant Book A, page 119

Bounded on the north by South Newport River, east by a large marsh. Plat shows tract bounded on the south by John Rutledge.

****

Deveaux, James and Bryan, Jonathan

400 acres, St. John Parish

Surveyed May 10, 1759   Plat Book C, page 21

Granted June 5, 1759   Grant Book B, page 153

Bounded on the north by Samuel Burnley and Phillipa Fenny, east by Josiah Powell.

****

Deveaux, William

500 acres, St. John Parish

Granted October 3, 1769   Grant Book G, page 428

Bounded on the northwest by said William Deveaux, southeast
by David Dicks.

****

Deveaux, William

500 acres, St. John Parish

Granted July 2, 1771   Grant Book I, page 361

Bounded on the southeast by said William Deveaux.

****

Dickinson, Paynter

250 acres, District of Midway

Granted December 6, 1757   Grant Book A, page 514

Bounded on the southeast by Collins Creek, northwest by Peter
Mackheigh.

****

Dicks, David

200 acres, St. John Parish

Granted May 21, 1762   Grant Book D, page 117

****

Dicks, David

200 acres, St. John Parish

Granted July 7, 1767   Grant Book F, page 289

****

Dicks, David

100 acres, St. John Parish

Granted July 7, 1767   Grant Book F, page 290

****

Dicks, David

500 acres, St. John Parish

Granted April 3, 1770   Grant Book G, page 574

Bounded on the west by John Oats and vacant land.

****

Dicks, David Jr.

50 acres, St. John Parish

Granted May 21, 1762   Grant Book D, page 118

****

Donnam, Daniel

550 acres, District of Newport

Granted April 5, 1757   Grant Book A, page 432

Bounded on the south by John Quarterman, Jr.

****

Donnam, William

100 acres, St. John Parish

Surveyed May 8, 1759   Plat Book C, page 52

Granted March 6, 1764   Grant Book D, page 403

Bounded on the south and west by Andrew Way and John Elliott,
northwest by said William Donnam, northeast by Elizabeth Simmons.

****

Donnavan, Daniel

500 acres, St. John Parish

Surveyed August 28, 1760   Plat Book C, page 52

Granted May 1, 1764   Grant Book E, page 7

Bounded on the south by John Davis.

****

Donnom, Daniel

500 acres, St. John Parish

Granted May 5, 1767   Grant Book F, page 224

Bounded on the south by Benjamin Andrew, east by John Humphreys
and Grey Elliott, northeast by Osgood and Joseph Way.

****

Donovan, Daniel

150 acres, St. John Parish

Surveyed October 21. 1760   Plat Book C, page 52

Granted July 3, 1764   Grant Book E, page 22

Bounded on the east by John Shave, south by Samuel Way.

****

Ducker, James

200 acres, St. John Parish

Surveyed August 16, 1762   Plat Book M, page 45

Granted March 6, 1764   Grant Book D, page 404

Bounded on the northeast by David Dicks and Israel Robinson.

****

Ducker, James

100 acres, St. John Parish

Granted February 6, 1770   Grant Book G, page 519

Bounded on the northwest by William Ducker.

****

Ducker, James

100 acres, St. John Parish

Surveyed July 21, 1769   Plat Book M, page 45

Granted February 6, 1770   Grant Book G, page 520

Bounded on the northwest by James Ducker.

****

Ducker, William

150 acres, St. John Parish

Granted February 6, 1770   Grant Book G, page 521

****

Dullea, Maurice

200 acres, District of Midway

Granted December 9, 1756   Grant Book A, page 376

****

Dunham, Daniel

500 acres, St. John Parish

Granted January 3, 1775   Grant Book M, page 870

Bounded on the southeast by James Stewart.

****

Dunham, James

250 acres, St. John Parish

Granted August 7, 1759   Grant Book B, page 536

Bounded on the east by John Sakmore, south by marshes of South
Newport River, west by Alex and Charles West.

****

Dunham, James and Denham, William

500 acres, District of Midway

Granted September 30, 1757 Grant Book A, page 568

Bounded on the east by John Davis and Parmenus Way, south by
said Davis and Way, west by David Stevens.

****

Dunham, William

500 acres, District of Newport

Granted September 30, 1757 Grant Book A, page 437

Bounded on the northwest by Elizabeth Simons, north by John
Elliott, east by Clement Martin and William Graves.

****

Dunham, William

200 acres, St. John Parish

Surveyed May 14, 1760   Plat Book C, page 52

Granted November 6, 1764 Grant Book E, page 61

Bounded on the north and west by Edward Way, north by said
William Dunham.

****

Dunham, William and Dunham, James

500 acres, District of Midway

Granted September 30, 1757   Grant Book A, page 568

Bounded on the east by John Davis and Parmenus Way, south by
said Davis and Way, west by David Stevens.

****

Elliot, John

600 acres, District of Newport

Granted March 5, 1756   Grant Book A, page 72

Bounded on the west by Andrew Way, north by Thomas Carter,
east by Clement Martin.

****

Elliott, Grey

300 acres, St. John Parish

Granted July 1, 1760   Grant Book B, page 427

Bounded on the east by Maurice Dullea.

****

Elliott, Grey

100 acres, St. John Parish

Granted June 5, 1759   Grant Book C, page 217

Bounded on the north by John Stuart and William Baker, south
by John Cain.

****

Elliott, Grey

300 acres, St. John Parish

Surveyed February 23, 1761   Plat Book C, page 59

Granted November 3, 1761   Grant Book C, page 264

Bounded on the east and south by Daniel Donnavan, John Shave, and Benjamin Farley.

****

Elliott, Grey

154 Acres, St. John Parish

Granted April 6, 1773   Grant Book I, page 942

Tract found on a resurvey to be the surplus quantity contained in the two tracts originally granted to Low and Andrews for 862 acres (See Grant Book I, page 942). Bounded on the southwest by land granted Andrews, southeast by land granted to Low.

****

Elliott, Grey and Gordon, John

100 acres, St. John Parish

Granted February 2, 1773   Grant Book I, page 902

Bounded on the east by Thomas Massey.

****

Elliott, Grey and Gordon, John

200 acres, St. John Parish

Granted August 6, 1765   Grant Book E, page 195

Tract heretofore ordered Scotton Davies, deceased, the said Grey Elliott and John Gordon being judgement creditors of Davies. Bounded on the east by Arthur Carney.

****

Elliott, Grey and Gordon, John

200 acres on Bermuda Island, St. John Parish

Surveyed March 21, 1761   Plat Book C, pag

Granted August 6, 1765   Grant Book E, pa

Formerly laid out for Daniel Mackay and by him
Elliott and Gordon. Bounded on the west by No
River, John Jones, and Heriott Crooke, south b
late Alexander Heron and John Barnaby. Origin
for Daniel McKay (Mackay), thence ordered to E
on April 3, 1764 (See Plat Book C, page 272).
Grey Elliott and John Gordon (See Grant Book E

****

Elliott, John

500 acres, District of Midway

Granted March 5, 1756   Grant Book A, pa

Bounded on the east by Isaac Lines and Andrew (

****

Elliott, John

300 acres, District of Newport

Granted March 5, 1756   Grant Book A, pag

Bounded on the east by said John Elliott.

****

Elliott, John

50 acres, District of Midway

Granted on the east by a branch of the Midway River, north
and west by Nathan Taylor.

****

Elliott, John

250 acres, St. John Parish

Granted December 4, 1759   Grant Book B, page 343

Bounded on the southeast and southwest by said John Elliott.

****

Elliott, John; Osgood, John; Stevens, John; Baker, William; Bacon, Joseph; Way, Parmenus; Quarterman, John; Winn, John; Graves, John; Baker, Richard (all trustees)

300 acres, District of Midway

Granted September 8, 1756   Grant Book A, page 327

Bounded on the west by Nathaniel Way. Land granted in trust for the use of the minister for the time being of the Dissenting or Congregational Church erected or to be erected in the District of Midway and Newport.

****

Elliott, William

500 acres, District of Newport

Granted June 7, 1757   Grant Book A, page 442

Bounded on the northwest and northeast by vacant land, west by Joseph Gibbons, southeast by John Mackintosh and marshes of South Newport River.

****

Elliott, William

500 acres, District of Newport

Granted September 8, 1756   Grant Book A, page 320

Bounded on the northwest by Charles West.

****

Elliott, William

100 acres, St. John Parish

Granted January 6, 1767   Grant Book F, page 18

Bounded on the southwest by said William Elliott.

****

Evans, Middleton

500 acres, District of Midway

Granted September 30, 1757   Grant Book A, page 454

Bounded on the southeast by a branch of the Midway River.

****

Farley, Benjamin

500 acres, District of Midway

Granted May 15, 1756   Grant Book A, page 190

Bounded on the east by Samuel Way, west by John Shave, south by John Mitchell and Joseph Massey.

****

Farley, Benjamin

350 acres, District of Newport

Granted February 11, 1757   Grant Book A, page 299

Bounded on the northwest by James Heart and Daniel McDonald.

****

Fenny, Philippa

500 acres, District of Newport

Granted April 5, 1757   Grant Book A, page 384

Bounded on the east by Samuel Burnley, south by Mathew Roche.

****

Fisher, James

250 acres, St. John Parish

Surveyed June 12, 1760   Plat Book C, page 62

Granted February 3, 1762   Grant Book D, page 29

Bounded on the northwest by Josiah Powell, northeast by William Baker.

****

Forbes, John

100 acres, St. John Parish

Granted January 7, 1772   Grant Book I, page 494

Bounded on the east by the north branch of River, north and west by Audley Maxwell.

****

Frink, Samuel

500 acres, St. John Parish

Granted May 7, 1771   Grant Book I, page 308

****

Frisbe, Josiah

100 acres, St. John Parish

Surveyed February 6, 1760   Plat Book C, page 62

Granted June 5, 1764   Grant Book E, page 15

Bounded on the north and northwest by William Johnson, southeast by John Burnet, northeast by Marshes of Newport River. Surveyed as Frisbe (See Plat Book C, page 62) and granted as Phrisby (See Grant Book E, page 15).

****

Gerardeau, Richard

250 acres, St. John Parish

Granted July 1, 1760   Grant Book B, page 524

Bounded on the south and west by James Mackay, north by Thomas
Way.

****

Gibbons, Joseph

600 acres, District of Newport

Granted December 9, 1756   Grant Book A, page 332

Bounded on the west by Samuel Hastings, south by a branch of
the Newport River.

****

Gibbons, Joseph

500 acres, District of Newport

Granted December 9, 1756   Grant Book A, page 333

Bounded on the east by Joseph Bacon and Sarah Mitchell, north
by John Mitchell and John Stevens.

****

Gibbons, Joseph

262 Acres, St. John Parish

Granted December 7, 1762   Grant Book D, page 261

Bounded on the south by said Joseph Gibbons, Elliott, and
Richard Hunt, west by Samuel Hastings, north by William Dunham
and William Graves.

****

Gibbons, Joseph

100 acres, St. John Parish

Granted October 1, 1771   Grant Book I, page 430

Bounded on the east by land of said Joseph Gibbons, northwest
by William Graves. Tract granted to_____Gibbons, executrix
and_____Gibbons, executor, in trust for Joseph Gibbons,
deceased, in trust for the eight heirs of Joseph Gibbons,
deceased.

****

Gibbons, William

530 acres, District of Newport

Granted December 9, 1756   Grant Book A, page 271

Bounded on the east by James Heart.

****

Girrardeaux, Isaac

500 acres, District of Newport

Granted March 28, 1758   Grant Book B, page 5

Bounded on the east by Andrew Way, west by Thomas Way.

****

Golding, John

200 acres, St. John Parish

Granted May 5, 1767   Grant Book F, page 231

Bounded on the north by Palmer Golding and Samuel Bacon, southwest by John Winn, east by said Palmer Golding, south by vacant
land. Tract is part of a tract of 300 acres of land heretofore
ordered Sarah Golding.

****

Golding, John

500 acres, St. John Parish

Surveyed August 30, 1759   Plat Book C, page 69

No grant recorded.

Bounded on the west by Francis Arthur and Edmund Tanant, north
by Edward McGaiur, east by William Lowe and John Gray, south
by Middleton Evans.

****

Golding, Palmer

200 acres, St. John Parish

Granted July 4, 1769   Grant Book G, page 358

Bounded on the north and east by Kenneth Baillie, south and
west by John Golding, northwest by Samuel Bacon.

****

Golding, Sarah

300 acres, St. John Parish

Surveyed March 29, 1760   Plat Book C, page 70

Granted December 3, 1760   Grant Book C, page 33

Bounded on the south by Robert Carr and Samuel Bacon, east by
John Winn, north by Thomas Carr.

****

Goldwire, Joseph

100 acres, St. John Parish

Surveyed January 15, 1770   Plat Book C, page 242

Granted December 3, 1771   Grant Book I, page 478

Originally surveyed for Charles Mearn, but ordered to Joseph
Goldwire (See Plat Book C, page 242). Granted to Joseph Goldwire.

****

Goodby, Joseph

400 acres, District of Newport

Granted September 8, 1756   Grant Book A, page 207

Bounded on the east by Moses Way, west by John Quarterman, Sr.

****

Gordon, John and Elliott, Grey

100 acres, St. John Parish

Granted February 2, 1773   Grant Book I, page 902

Bounded on the east by Thomas Massey.

****

Gordon, John and Elliott, Grey

200 acres, St. John Parish

Granted August 6, 1765   Grant Book E, page 195

Tract heretofore ordered Scotton Davies, deceased, the said Grey Elliott and John Gordon being judgement creditors of Davies. Bounded on the east by Arthur Carney.

****

Gordon, John and Elliott, Grey

200 acres on Bermuda Island, St. John Parish

Surveyed March 21, 1761   Plat Book C, page 272

Granted August 6, 1765   Grant Book E, page 196

Formerly laid out for Daniel Mackay and by him morgaged to Elliott and Gordon. Bounded on the west by North Newport River, John Jones, and Heriott Crooke, south by estate of the late Alexander Heron and John Barnabe. Originally surveyed for Daniel Mackay, thence ordered to Elliott and Gordon on April 3, 1764 (See Plat Book C, page 272). Granted to Grey Elliott and John Gordon (See Grant Book E, page 196).

****

Graham, James

1000 acres, St. John Parish

Granted July 3, 1770   Grant Book I, page 49

Bounded partly on the northwest by said James Graham and partly
by vacant land, northeast by his Excellency James Wright, on
all other sides by vacant land.

****

Graham, James

1000 acres, St. John Parish

Granted July 3, 1770   Grant Book I, page 50

Bounded on the northwest by Nathaniel Hall, partly southeast
by said James Graham, all other sides by vacant land.

****

Graham, John

700 acres, District of Newport

Granted February 7, 1758   Grant Book A, page 603

Bounded on the south by Newport River, east by Robert Bailey,
southwest by Robert Noble, east by George Noble.

****

Graham, John

1000 acres, St. John Parish

Granted April 2, 1771   Grant Book I, page 282

Bounded on the northwest by Canoochee River, northeast by Joseph
Butler, southwest by Thomas Shruder.

****

Graves, John

500 acres on the head of Newport River

Granted February 5, 1757   Grant Book A, page 296

Bounded on the east by Alexander Low, west by William Graves, north by Newport River.

****

Graves, John

300 acres, St. John Parish

Surveyed May 2, 1760   Plat Book C, page 69

Granted February 3, 1762   Grant Book D, page 27

Bounded on the northeast by William Lowe.

****

Graves, John; Osgood, John; Stevens, John; Elliott, John;
Baker, William; Bacon, Joseph; Way, Parmenus; Quarterman, John;
Winn, John; Baker, Richard (all trustees)

300 acres, District of Midway

Granted September 8, 1756   Grant Book A, page 327

Bounded on the west by Nathaniel Way. Land granted in trust
for the use of the minister for the time being of the Dissenting
or Congregational Church erected or to be erected in the District
of Midway and Newport.

****

Graves, William

500 acres at the head of Newport River

Granted September 8, 1756   Grant Book A, page 269

Bounded on the east by John Graves, west by John Stewart, Jr.

****

Graves, William

600 acres, District of Newport

Granted December 9, 1756   Grant Book A, page 270

Bounded on the south by William Martin.

****

Graves, William

200 acres, District of Newport

Granted September 30, 1757   Grant Book A, page 453

Bounded on the south and east by Benjamin Andrew, west by
John Humphrey.

****

Graves, William

150 acres, St. John Parish

Granted August 2, 1774   Grant Book M, page 194

Bounded on the west by said William Graves, east by Joseph
Gibbons, southwest by William Quarterman.

****

Green, Jeremiah

100 acres, St. John Parish

Granted July 1, 1760   Grant Book D, page 332

Bounded on the north by Glebe land, southeast by Samuel Burnley.

****

Green, John

500 acres, District of Midway

Granted January 16, 1756   Grant Book A, page 130

Bounded on the west by a branch of the Midway River called
Collins Creek and Thomas Goldsmith, north by Nathaniel Watson.

****

Hall, Lyman and Miller, Samuel

300 acres, St. John Parish

Granted April 13, 1761   Grant Book G, page 261

Bounded on the southeast by Robert Smallwood.

****

Hall, Nathaniel

1000 acres, St. John Parish

Granted January 2, 1770   Grant Book G, page 500

****

Hamilton, Henry

100 acres, St. John Parish

Surveyed April 26, 1753   Plat Book C, page 83

Granted January 16, 1756   Grant Book A, page 16

Tract located on the south side of the Midway River. Bounded on the southeast by John Baillou, southwest by John Calkins, northeast by marshes of Midway River.

****

Harkins, Charles

300 acres, St. John Parish

Granted May 3, 1763   Grant Book D, page 305

****

Harley, James

100 acres, St. John Parish

Surveyed February 25, 1760   Plat Book C, page 79

Granted September 7, 1762   Grant Book D, page 200

Bounded on the northwest by said James Harley, northeast by Nathaniel Way, southeast by vacant land, on every other side by Samuel Burnley.

****

Harley, James

100 acres, District of Midway

Granted June 7, 1757   Grant Book A, page 416

Bounded on the north by Nathaniel Way, southwest by Samuel
Burnley.

****

Harris, Francis

1500 acres, St. John Parish

Granted September 5, 1769   Grant Book G, page 412

****

Harvey, Emanuel

100 acres, St. John Parish

Granted June 7, 1774   Grant Book I, page 1042

Bounded on the southeast by lands surveyed for Middleton Evans
and William Johnson, partly northwest by Francis Brown, on all
other sides by vacant land.

****

Harvey, Emanuel

100 acres, St. John Parish

Granted June 7, 1774   Grant Book I, page 1055

Bounded on the northeast by land originally Middleton Evans,
northwest by said grantee, southwest by Messieurs Odingsell
and Tannat, southeast by land originally Francis Arthur.

****

Hastings, Samuel

750 acres, District of Newport

Granted December 6, 1757   Grant Book A, page 510

Tract located on South Newport River. Bounded on the west
by James Heart.

****

Hazzard, Richard Jr.

500 acres, St. John Parish

Granted May 5, 1767   Grant Book F, page 233

Bounded on the east by a creek and marshes of Midway River, northeast by land alloted William Balleau and Edmund Tannatt, west by land surveyed for Edward McGuire, southwest partly by land since surveyed for William Johnson and partly by land also vacant at the time of the survey. Tract was originally alloted to the said Richard Hazzard by the late president and assistants of our province aforesaid.

****

Heart, James

550 acres, District of Newport

Granted September 8, 1756   Grant Book A, page 198

Bounded on the northeast by Samuel Hastings.

****

Holzendorff, Frederick

50 acres, St. John Parish

Granted November 2, 1762   Grant Book D, page 226

Bounded on the west by John Lupton, south by Edward Way, east by John Elliott.

****

Holzendorff, Frederick

200 acres, St. John Parish

Granted November 2, 1762   Grant Book D, page 227

Bounded on the southeast by William Low.

****

Holzendorff, Frederick

200 acres, St. John Parish

Surveyed July 7, 1761   Plat Book C, page 79

No grant recorded.

Bounded on the southeast by Benjamin Baker.

****

Hughes, Philip

300 acres, St. John Parish

Granted January 5, 1768   Grant Book G, page 8

Tract was heretofore ordered to and surveyed for George Godfrey
(See Grant Book G, page 8). Survey not recorded.

****

Huginen, David

300 acres, St. John Parish

Granted August 6, 1771   Grant Book I, page 384

Bounded on the southeast by land granted, partly northeast and
partly northwest by said David Huginen, south by Robert Miller
and vacant land, on all other sides by vacant lands.

****

Humphry, John

400 acres, District of Newport

Granted February 7, 1758   Grant Book A, page 565

Bounded on the south by Elizabeth Baker and Richard Baker.

****

Hunt, Richard

100 acres, St. John Parish

Surveyed July 14, 1759   Plat Book C, page 78

No grant recorded.

****

Irvine, John

500 acres, St. John Parish

Surveyed February 2, 1771   Plat Book C, page 102

Granted April 2, 1771   Grant Book I, page 286

****

Jervey, David

150 acres, St. John Parish

Granted May 1, 1759   Grant Book B, page 191

Bounded on the south by David Stephens.

****

Johnson, Lewis

500 acres, District of Midway

Granted January 16, 1756   Grant Book A, page 58

Bounded on the west by Oliver Shaw and John Baillou, north by marshes of Midway River, east by James Ellison.

****

Johnson, Lewis

100 acres, District of Midway

Granted January 16, 1756   Grant Book A, page 60

Bounded on the west by John Balliou, north by marshes of Midway River, east by said Lewis Johnson.

Johnson, William

50 acres, St. John Parish

Granted July 1, 1760   Grant Book B, page 398

Bounded on the north by Richard Hazzard, west by said William
Johnson.

****

Johnson, William

100 acres, St. John Parish

Surveyed December 12, 1758   Plat Book C, page 102

Granted August 7, 1759   Grant Book B, page 453

Bounded on the northeast by Richard Hazzard.

****

Johnson, William Martin

500 acres on a branch of Midway River called Collins Creek.

Granted January 16, 1756   Grant Book A, page 57

Bounded on the southeast by marshes of Collins Creek and land
of James Butler. Tract located either in Great Ogeechee District
or District of Midway.

****

Jones, John

200 acres, St. John Parish

Surveyed October 22, 1760   Plat Book C, page 103

Granted April 13, 1761   Grant Book C, page 61

Bounded on the east by Grey Elliott.

****

Jones, William

400 acres, St. John Parish

Surveyed April 12, 1773   Plat Book C, page 103

Granted August 2, 1774   Grant Book M, page 212

Bounded on the north by John Stevens, Joseph Oswell, and William Bacon, east by William Bacon and Thomas Young, south by William Jones, west by William Jones and Mary Stevens. Tract surveyed as 500 acres and granted as 400 acres.

****

Kelsal, Roger

150 acres, St. John Parish

Granted March 7, 1775   Grant Book M, page 1079

Bounded on the southwest and northwest by vacant land, northeast by Roger Kelsal, southeast by Peacock.

****

Kelsall, Roger

150 acres, St. John Parish

Granted February 7, 1775   Grant Book M, page 1011

Bounded on the north by Silvanus Robertson, east by Duckers, west by David Decks.

****

Lawrence, Nicholas

50 acres, St. John Parish

Granted July 4, 1758   Grant Book A, page 663

Bounded on the north by marsh of Midway River, south and east by James Maxwell, Jr.

****

Lawrence, Nicholas

300 acres, St. John Parish

Granted July 4, 1758   Grant Book A, page 665

Bounded on the north by a creek leading from the Midway River,
south by vacant land, east by Henry Hamilton, west by James
Maxwell, Jr.

****

Lawson, John

100 acres, St. John Parish

Granted July 1, 1760   Grant Book B, page 440

Bounded on the north by a creek, west by William Hester.

****

Lawson, John

200 acres, St. John Parish

Surveyed May 12, 1760   Plat Book C, page 157

Granted April 13, 1761   Grant Book D, page 366

Bounded on the south by North Newport River, east by William
Carr, north by Edward McGuire, west by William Low.

****

LeConte, William

500 acres, St. Andrew and St. John Parishes

Surveyed August 31, 1770   Plat Book C, page 161

Granted December 4, 1770   Grant Book I, page 221

****

60

LeConte, William

300 acres, St. John Parish

Granted November 1, 1774   Grant Book M, page 682

****

Lee, Thomas

200 acres, St. John Parish

Surveyed January 7, 1760   Plat Book C, page 158

Granted April 13, 1761   Grant Book C, page 160

Bounded on the southeast by Isaac Tripp, northeast by Jonathan
Bryan.

****

Lewis, Benjamin

100 acres, St. John Parish

Surveyed January 2, 1766   Plat Book C, page 157

Granted November 4, 1766   Grant Book E, page 392

Bounded on the northeast by Thomas Quarterman and Richard
Spencer, west by Grey Elliott, south by William Graves, southeast by Adam Bosomworth.

****

Lewis, Jacob

250 acres, St. John Parish

Granted December 4, 1770   Grant Book I, page 222

Bounded on the southwest by James McKay, northwest by James
Stewart, east by Edward Way and vacant land, south by Nathaniel
Clark.

****

Liddle, William

200 acres, St. John Parish

Surveyed November 18, 1761   Plat Book C, page 156

Granted August 3, 1762   Grant Book D, page 171

Bounded on the northeast by William Baker.

****

Lines, Isaac

500 acres, District of Midway

Surveyed May 24, 1750   Plat Book C, page 166

Granted December 9, 1756   Grant Book A, page 239

Tract known as Bideford, bounded on the east by Audley
Maxwell.

****

Lockerman, Jacob

350 acres, District of Midway

Granted December 6, 1757   Grant Book A, page 660

Bounded on the east by a branch of the St. Catherine River,
south by George Cubbidge.

****

Love, George

500 acres on Newport River

Granted December 9, 1756   Grant Book A, page 370

Bounded on the west by Mrs. St. Julian, north by Newport River,
east and south by Clement Martin. Tract located either in St.
John Parish or St. Andrew Parish.

****

Low, William

600 acres, St. John Parish

Granted March 5, 1756 Grant Book C, page 156

****

Low, William

500 acres, St. John Parish

Granted August 7, 1759 Grant Book B, page 134

Bounded on the north by Newport River, west by lands planted by Benjamin Andrews.

****

Low, William

600 acres, District of Midway, St. John Parish

Granted August 7, 1759 Grant Book B, page 135

****

Lupton, John

800 acres, District of Midway

Granted January 16, 1756 Grant Book A, page 76

Bounded on the south by John Stevens, west by Samuel Way, east by Edward Way, northwest by John Elliott.

****

Lynn, John

200 acres, St. John Parish

Surveyed April 4, 1761 Plat Book C, page 156

Granted February 7, 1764 Grant Book D, page 383

Bounded on the southeast by pond of Lachlan McIntosh.

****

Lynn, John

150 acres, St. John Parish

Surveyed December 27, 1765   Plat Book C, page 157

Granted April 5, 1768   Grant Book G, page 76

Tract located on a neck of North Newport River, bounded on the
north by Thomas White, west by Donald McKay, southeast by said
John Lynn.

****

Lynn, Thomas

2000 acres, St. John Parish

Surveyed April 23, 1774   Plat Book C, page 157

Granted May 3, 1774   Grant Book I, page 1007

****

Mackay, Angus

150 acres, District of Newport

Surveyed November 19, 1755   Plat Book C, page 228

Granted December 6, 1757   Grant Book A, page 505

Tract located on South Branch, North Newport River, bounded
on the east by Donald McDonald. Tract surveyed as McKay and
granted as Mackay.

****

Mackay, Donald

250 acres, District of Newport

Granted February 11, 1757   Grant Book A, page 308

Tract located on Boyn Creek.

****

Mackay, James

650 acres at the head of Newport River

Surveyed March 8, 1755   Plat Book C, page 268

Granted September 8, 1756   Grant Book A, page 314

****

Mackay, James

500 acres, District of Newport

Granted April 5, 1757   Grant Book A, page 377

Bounded on the west by Thomas Smith, east by said James Mackay.

****

Mackintosh, Donald

200 acres, District of Newport

Granted September 30, 1757   Grant Book A, page 474

Tract located on South Branch, South Newport River.

****

Mackintosh, Lachlan

500 acres, District of Newport

Surveyed September 11, 1754   Plat Book C, page 172

Granted February 11, 1757   Grant Book A, page 311

Bounded on the northeast by marshes of Newport River. Surveyed as McIntosh and granted as Mackintosh.

****

Mackintosh, William

500 acres, District of Newport

Surveyed September 12, 1754   Plat Book C, page 173

Granted February 11, 1757   Grant Book A, page 310

Tract known as Garthmore, bounded on the northeast by Newport River, southeast by Lacklin Macintosh.

****

Magee, Thomas

100 acres, St. John Parish

Surveyed March 21, 1759   Plat Book C, page 250

Granted July 1, 1760   Grant Book B, page 527

Bounded on the north by John Pearson, east by a creek.

****

Mallard, Lazarus

100 acres, St. John Parish

Granted November 1, 1774   Grant Book M, page 705

Bounded on the east by Robert Mallard.

****

Mann, Luke

100 acres, St. John Parish

Surveyed November 25, 1767   Plat Book C, page 228

Granted March 7, 1769   Grant Book G, page 283

Bounded on the southwest by David Dicks, southeast by Sylvanus Robinson.

****

Mann, Luke

100 acres, St. John Parish

Granted July 4, 1769   Grant Book G, page 362

****

Martin, Clement

500 acres, District of Newport

Granted March 5, 1756   Grant Book A, page 92

Tract located on the south side of North Branch, Newport River, bounded on the north by Newport River, south by William Martin and vacant land, west by Thomas Carter and vacant land. Tract known as Rochelle.

****

Martin, Clement

500 acres, District of Newport

Granted March 5, 1756   Grant Book A, page 93

Tract located on the south side of Newport River, bounded on the north by said Clement Martin. Tract known as Windsor.

****

Martin, Clement

500 acres, St. John Parish

Granted May 4, 1773   Grant Book I, page 1002

****

Martin, James Donnon

100 acres, St. John Parish

Granted February 7, 1775   Grant Book M, page 1020

Bounded on the north and east by John Martin, east by Elizabeth Simmon.

****

Martin, John

84 acres, St. John Parish

Surveyed August 22, 1770   Plat Book C, page 275

Granted February 5, 1771   Grant Book H, page 52

Bounded on the north by Thomas Carter and land belonging to the estate of Joseph Gibbons, deceased, west by land of said grantee, southwest by McLocklan and land of said grantee, south by said grantee.

****

Martin, John

100 acres, St. John Parish

Surveyed May 6, 1772   Plat Book C, page 294

No grant recorded.

Bounded on the east by Elizabeth Simmons and John Martin.

****

Massey, Joseph

500 acres, District of Newport

Surveyed November 25, 1755   Plat Book C, page 227

Granted April 5, 1757   Grant Book A, page 388

Bounded on the east by John Mitchell, north by Benjamin Farley, west by Robert Smallwood.

****

Massey, Joseph

200 acres, St. John Parish

Surveyed July 2, 1759   Plat Book C, page 227

Granted April 13, 1761   Grant Book D, page 374

****

Massey, Joseph

100 acres, St. John Parish

Surveyed February 20, 1761   Plat Book C, page 404

No grant recorded.

Bounded on the northeast by Thomas Massey.

****

Massey, Joseph

100 acres, St. John Parish

Surveyed February 20, 1761   Plat Book C, page 221

No grant recorded.

Bounded on the northeast by Joseph Massey

****

Maxwell, Audley

350 acres, District of Midway

Surveyed June 9, 1755   Plat Book C, page 262

Granted March 5, 1756   Grant Book A, page 191

****

Maxwell, Audley

500 acres, District of Midway

Surveyed May 22, 1750   Plat Book C, page 167

Granted September 8, 1756   Grant Book A, page 196

Tract known as Limerick, bounded on the east by a branch of Midway River, west by Isaac Lines.

****

Maxwell, Audley

150 acres, District of Midway

Surveyed March 30, 1757   Plat Book C, page 211

Granted September 30, 1757 Grant Book A, page 443

Bounded on the south by Kenneth Bailey, west by Audley Maxwell, Jr., north by said Audley Maxwell, east by marsh land.

****

Maxwell, Audley

350 acres, St. John Parish

Surveyed October 4, 1757   Plat Book C, page 254

Granted July 7, 1761   Grant Book C, page 333

Bounded on the north by Matthew Roche, east by Josiah Powell.

****

Maxwell, Audley Jr.

200 acres, District of Midway

Granted September 8, 1756 Grant Book A, page 197

Bounded on the north by Audley Maxwell, Sr. and Isaac Lines, west by Andrew Collins and Samuel Bacon.

****

Maxwell, James Jr.

690 acres, St. John Parish

Surveyed April 4, 1767   Plat Book C, page 269

Granted July 5, 1768   Grant Book G, page 138

Bounded on the southeast by Nicholas Lawrence, northwest by Nathaniel Way, north by salt marsh.

****

Maxwell, Thomas

850 acres, St. John Parish

Granted August 3, 1762   Grant Book D, page 157

Bounded on the north by Midway River and marshes thereof, north-west by Lewis Johnson.

****

McDonald, Donald

200 acres at the head of the South Branch, South Newport River

Granted April 5, 1757   Grant Book A, page 433

Tract became either St. John Parish or St. Andrew Parish in 1758.

****

McGuire, Edward

250 acres, St. John Parish

Surveyed February 14, 1759   Plat Book C, page 220

Granted August 7, 1759   Grant Book B, page 435

Bounded on the east by Richard Hazard, north by Edmund Tannatt, south by William Johnston.

****

McGuire, Joseph

200 acres, District of Newport, St. John Parish

Granted February 7, 1758   Grant Book B, page 450

Bounded on the south by Newport River, west by George Noble, northeast by William Low.

****

McIntosh, George

400 acres, St. John and St. Andrew Parshes

Granted September 6, 1774. Grant Book M, page 350

Bounded on the north by land run for John McIntosh and William Elliott, west by land run for Joseph Gibbons, south by land run for Robert Stuart and William Norton, east by vacant marsh.

****

McIntosh, John

300 acres, District of Newport

Surveyed August 28, 1755   Plat Book C, page 237

Granted May 1, 1759   Grant Book B, page 101

****

McIntosh, Lachlan (of Darien)

500 acres, St. John Parish

Granted October 4, 1774   Grant Book M, page 577

Bounded on the north and northeast by vacant land and marshes, east by land run for George McIntosh and John McIntosh, south by South Newport River.

****

McIntosh, Roderick

500 acres, St. John Parish

Surveyed March 21, 1754   Plat Book M, page 69

Granted December 4, 1759   Grant Book B, page 287

Bounded on the southwest by Henry Calwell, north by vacant land, on every other side by marshes of the Rivers Sapelo and Newport. Even though this tract was granted as being in St. John Parish, it may have been in St. Andrew Parish (See Plat Book M, page 69).

McKay, Daniel

200 acres, St. John Parish

Surveyed March 21, 1761   Plat Book C, page 403

No grant recorded

Bounded on the south by John Barnaby, east by Newport River and John Jones, north by Alexander Herons.

****

McKay, Elizabeth Ann

177 acres, St. John Parish

Granted February 7, 1775   Grant Book M, page 1025

Bounded on the south by John Perkins, east by Charles Waters and Mr. Butterfield, north by Colonel Heron, west by Herriott Crooke and John Witherspoon.

****

McLeod, Roderick

200 acres, District of Newport

Surveyed January 7, 1756   Plat Book C, page 254

Granted February 3, 1767   Grant Book F, page 70

Bounded on the southwest by John McIntosh. Tract surveyed as being in St. Andrew Parish and for Roderick McCloud.

****

McPherson, John

250 acres, St. John Parish

Surveyed October 8, 1759   Plat Book C, page 401

No grant recorded.

Bounded on the northwest by Thomas Christers, north by Josiah Powell.

****

McPherson, William

200 acres, St. John Parish

Surveyed February 20, 1760   Plat Book C, pages 247 and 404

Granted September 2, 1766   Grant Book E, page 356

Bounded on the east by said William McPherson and Parmenas Way.

****

Mearn, Charles

100 acres, St. John Parish

Surveyed January 15, 1770   Plat Book C, page 242

Granted December 3, 1771   Grant Book I, page 478

Originally surveyed for Charles Mearn, thence ordered to Joseph Goldwire (See Plat Book C, page 242). Granted to Joseph Gold-wire (See Grant Book I, page 478).

****

Midway, Inhabitants of

11 acres (½ of an island), St. John Parish

Surveyed August 21, 1760   Plat Book C, pages 218 and 402

No grant recorded.

Plot of about 11 acres of land granted the inhabitants of Midway for a landing place being one moiety of an island containing about 22 acres (See Plat Book C, page 402).

****

Miller, Robert

300 acres, St. John Parish

Surveyed February 19, 1762   Plat Book C, page 236

Granted February 5, 1765   Grant Book E, page 106

Bounded on the northwest by James Bratcher and said Robert Miller.

****

Miller, Robert

200 acres, St. John Parish

Surveyed August 15, 1761   Plat Book C, page 217

Granted February 5, 1765   Grant Book E, page 107

Bounded on the east by Maurice Dulea, northwest by James Bratcher and vacant land.

****

Miller, Samuel and Hall, Lyman

300 acres, St. John Parish

Granted April 13, 1761   Grant Book G, page 261

Bounded on the southeast by Robert Smallwood.

****

Mills, William

150 acres, District of Newport

Granted December 9, 1756   Grant Book A, page 246

****

Mills, William

100 acres, St. John Parish

Surveyed April 18, 1759   Plat Book C, page 250

Granted December 4, 1759   Grant Book B, page 316

Bounded on the southwest by said William Mills, east by John Quarterman.

****

Mills, William

250 acres, St. John Parish

Surveyed June 8, 1761   Plat Book C, pages 252 and 401

Granted November 3, 1761   Grant Book C, page 252

Bounded on the northeast and southeast by said William Mills,
west by Benjamin Baker and Thomas Mills.

****

Mitchell, Francis

550 acres, St. John Parish

Granted November 2, 1762   Grant Book D, page 230

Bounded on the southeast by William Gibbons.

****

Mitchell, Francis

350 acres, St. John Parish

Surveyed January 28, 1762   Plat Book C, page 248

No grant recorded.

Bounded on the southeast by William Graves.

****

Mitchell, John

500 acres, District of Midway

Granted September 8, 1756   Grant Book A, page 211

Bounded on the east by John Stevens.

****

Mitchell, John

146 acres, St. John Parish

Granted April 13, 1761   Grant Book D, page 17

Bounded on the southeast by John Stewart, north by Audley Maxwell.

****

Mitchell, John

400 acres, St. John Parish

Surveyed January 3, 1766   Plat Book C, page 247

Granted September 6, 1768   Grant Book G, page 184

Tract located on a swamp about three miles above Millers cowpen.

****

Mitchell, John

200 acres, St. John Parish

Surveyed September 7, 1770   Plat Book C, page 275

No grant recorded.

****

Mitchell, John

200 acres, St. John Parish

Surveyed September 6, 1770   Plat Book C, page 274

No grant recorded.

Bounded on the southeast by Spencer, south and southeast by John Mitchell.

****

Mitchell, Sarah

500 acres, District of Newport

Granted September 8, 1756   Grant Book A, page 272

Bounded on the southwest by Mr. Osgood.

****

Montgomery, James

100 acres, St. John Parish

Surveyed December 20, 1759   Plat Book C, page 410

****

Moran, Charles

350 acres, St. John Parish

Surveyed September 9, 1768   Plat Book C, page 223

Granted November 1, 1768   Grant Book G, page 213

Bounded on the west by said Charles Moran and vacant land.

****

Mulryne, John

500 acres, St. John Parish

Granted July 4, 1758   Grant Book B, page 42

Bounded on the north by Captain Mark Carr, south by Middleton
Evans, east by marshes and creeks of Midway River.

****

Netherclift, Thomas

1000 acres, St. John Parish

Granted February 7, 1775   Grant Book M, page 1037

Bounded on the northeast by William Wylly.

****

Noble, George

100 acres, District of Newport, St. John Parish

Granted October 2, 1759   Grant Book D, page 76

Bounded on the south by North Newport River.

****

Noble, Robert

100 acres, District of Newport, St. John Parish

Granted October 2, 1759   Grant Book D, page 77

Bounded on the northwest by William Thomas, northeast by vacant land, on every other side by Newport River.

****

Norton, William

200 acres, District of Newport

Granted December 6, 1757   Grant Book A, page 507

Bounded on the south by South Newport River, west by Robert Stewart.

****

Odensall, Charles

200 acres, St. John Parish

Granted June 5, 1770   Grant Book I, page 28

Bounded on the southwest by Edward McGuire, southeast by Edward Jamnett.

****

Osgood, John

100 acres, District of Midway

Granted December 6, 1757   Grant Book A, page 546

Bounded on the east by said John Osgood and Edward Way.

****

Osgood, John (Reverend)

500 acres, District of Newport

Granted October 31, 1755   Grant Book A, page 65

Bounded on the north by Edward Way and John Stevens.

****

Osgood, John (Reverend)

500 acres, District of Midway

Granted October 31, 1755   Grant Book A, page 66

Bounded on the east and south by John Quarterman, Sr.

****

Osgood, John; Stevens, John; Elliott, John; Baker, William;
Bacon, Joseph; Way, Parmenus; Quarterman, John; Winn, John;
Graves, John; Baker, Richard (all trustees)

300 acres, District of Midway

Granted September 8, 1756   Grant Book A, page 327

Bounded on the west by Nathaniel Way. Land granted in trust
for the use of the minister for the time being of the Dissenting
or Congregational Church erected or to be erected in the District
of Midway and Newport.

****

Osgood, Josiah

500 acres, District of Newport

Granted March 5, 1756   Grant Book A, page 71

Bounded on the northeast by Richard Spencer.

****

Oswald, Joseph; Oswald, Mary; Oswald, Sarah

500 acres on North Branch, Newport River

Granted May 15, 1756   Grant Book A, page 176

Bounded on the northwest by John Stevens, southeast by Joseph Way.

****

Oswald, Mary; Oswald, Joseph; Oswald, Sarah

500 acres on North Branch, Newport River

Granted May 15, 1756   Grant Book A, page 176

Bounded on the northwest by John Stevens, southeast by Joseph Way.

****

Oswald, Sarah; Oswald, Joseph; Oswald, Mary

500 acres on North Branch, Newport River

Granted May 15, 1756   Grant Book A, page 176

Bounded on the northwest by John Stevens, southeast by Joseph Way.

****

Oswell, Joseph

100 acres, St. John Parish

Granted June 5, 1771   Grant Book I, page 348

Bounded on the west by said grantee.

****

Outerbridge, White

500 acres, District of Newport

Granted April 5, 1757   Grant Book A, page 379

Bounded on the northeast and southeast by William Gibbons and John Honneur.

****

Parker, John

500 acres, District of Midway

Granted March 5, 1756   Grant Book A, page 140

Bounded on the east by Peter Mackhugh.

****

Peacock, Thomas

250 acres, District of Newport

Granted October 31, 1755   Grant Book A, page 84

Tract located between the forks of Newport River, bounded on the northeast and southwest by Newport River, northwest by William Peacock.

****

Peacock, Thomas

100 acres on north side of South Branch, North Newport River

Granted March 5, 1756   Grant Book A, page 180

****

Peacock, Thomas

200 acres, St. John Parish

Granted September 1, 1767   Grant Book F, page 362

Bounded on the south by Benjamin Andrew, William Graves, and William Wilson, west by William Wilson and Grey Elliott, northeast by John Stewart and land surveyed for William Bacon, east by Benjamin Lewis and Benjamin Andrew.

****

Peacock, Thomas

78 acres, St. John Parish

Granted September 1, 1767   Grant Book F, page 363

Bounded on the northwest partly by Josiah Osgood and partly
by William Clifton, south by North Newport River, east and
northeast by William Peacock, James Read, and said Thomas
Peacock.

****

Peacock, William

100 acres, District of Newport

Granted November 7, 1755   Grant Book A, page 88

Tract located between the forks of the Newport River, bounded
on the west by William Clifton and Josiah Osgood, east by
Thomas Peacock.

****

Peacock, William

150 acres, St. John Parish

Granted March 3, 1772   Grant Book I, page 540

Bounded on the east by Benjamin Baker, partly south by Benjamin
Baker and Holsondorff, on all other sides by vacant land.

****

Perkins, Thomas

200 acres, St. John Parish

Granted March 3, 1767   Grant Book F, page 140

Bounded on the west by Mary Stevens, east by Joshua Clark, south
by John Barnabe, southeast by Half Moon Bluff on North Newport
River.

****

Perkins, Thomas

50 acres, St. John Parish

Granted August 5, 1774   Grant Book H, page 106

Bounded on the northwest by Thompson, southwest by Robert Noble, southeast by marshes of North Newport River.

****

Phrisby, Josiah

100 acres, St. John Parish

Surveyed February 6, 1760   Plat Book C, page 62

Granted June 5, 1764   Grant Book E, page 15

Bounded on the north and northwest by William Johnson, southeast by John Burnet, northeast by marshes of Newport River. Surveyed as Josiah Frisbe and granted as Josiah Phrisby.

****

Plummer, Nathaniel

450 acres, St. John Parish

Granted December 4, 1770   Grant Book I, page 224

Bounded on the northwest by Joseph Massey, southeast by land ordered Grey Elliott, partly northeast by vacant land and partly by John Elliott, on all other sides by vacant land.

****

Powell, Josiah

460 acres, District of Midway, St. John Parish

Granted July, 1760   Grant Book C, page 172

Bounded on the east by William, north by Sam Burnley.

****

Powell, Josiah

264 acres, St. John Parish

Granted February 7, 1775   Grant Book M, page 1039

Bounded on the northwest by Robert Miller, northeast by David Stephens, southeast by Maurice Dullea, southwest by Grey Elliott.

****

Pritchard, James

150 acres, District of Newport

Granted December 6, 1757   Grant Book A, page 506

Bounded on the west and south by Edward Macguire, north by Newport River.

****

Pryce, Charles Jr.

500 acres, St. John Parish

Granted June 2, 1772   Grant Book I, page 638

****

Quarterman, John

300 acres, St. John Parish

Granted December 3, 1760   Grant Book C, page 178

Bounded on the southwest by John Graves.

****

Quarterman, John

150 acres, St. John Parish

Granted July 1, 1760   Grant Book B, page 438

Bounded on the south by said John Quarterman, west by John Quarterman, Jr., east by Parmenus Way.

****

Quarterman, John Sr.

500 acres, District of Midway

Granted March 5, 1756   Grant Book A, page 171

Bounded on the east by Nathan Taylor, south by Isaac Lines.

****

Quarterman, Rebeckah

300 acres, District of Newport

Granted March 5, 1756   Grant Book B, page 17

Bounded on the southeast by Joseph Winn, southwest by Richard Spencer, northwest by Sarah Mitchel, east by Joseph Winn.

****

Quarterman, William

350 acres, St. John Parish

Granted December 3, 1760   Grant Book B, page 537

Bounded on the south by Thomas Way, north by John and William Graves, east by Isaac Gerardeau.

****

Read, James

637 acres on North Branch, Newport River

Granted May 15, 1756   Grant Book A, page 127

Bounded on the north by Thomas and William Carr, east by Oliver Shaw, northwest by Edmund Tannatt, southwest by Newport River.

****

Read, James

275 acres, District of Newport

Granted February 11, 1757   Grant Book A, page 301

Bounded on the northwest by said James Read, east by Oliver Shaw.
****

Robinson, Silvanus

250 acres, St. John Parish

Surveyed May 1, 1761   Plat Book C, page 420

Granted May 21, 1762   Grant Book D, page 110

Bounded on the east by James Taylor, northwest by David Dicks.

****

Robinson, Sylvanus

100 acres, St. John Parish

Granted April 3, 1764   Grant Book D, page 413

Bounded on the north by said Sylvanus Robinson.

****

Robinson, Sylvanus

100 acres, St. John Parish

Granted July 7, 1767   Grant Book F, page 302

Bounded on the northeast partly by David Dicks, Sr. and partly
by vacant land.

****

Robinson, Sylvanus

100 acres, St. John Parish

Granted October 6, 1772   Grant Book I, page 775

****

Rose, Alexander

250 acres, District of Newport

Granted December 6, 1757   Grant Book A, page 586

Tract located between the North and South Branches of the Newport
River.

****

Ryan, Daniel

100 acres, St. John Parish

Surveyed January 29, 1761   Plat Book C, page 421

Granted May 21, 1762   Grant Book D, page 136

Bounded on the west by Lattimore, southeast by Carlile, east by salt marsh.

****

Sallen, Robert

200 acres, St. John Parish

Surveyed February 15, 1773   Plat Book C, page 357

Granted July 5, 1774   Grant Book M, page 102

Bounded on the southwest by Robert Sallen.

****

Sallens, Peter

250 acres, St. John Parish

Surveyed March 31, 1767   Plat Book C, page 302

Granted March 1, 1768   Grant Book G, page 61

Bounded on the southeast by Lynn, west by Thomas Young, north by surveyed land.

****

Salters, Samuel

200 acres, St. John Parish

Granted November 1, 1774   Grant Book M, page 739

****

Saltus, Henry

200 acres, St. John Parish

Surveyed December 14, 1761   Plat Book C, page 296

No grant recorded.

Bounded on the southwest by Parminus Way.

****

Sandiford, John

200 acres, St. John Parish

Granted November 4, 1766   Grant Book E, page 401

Bounded on the west by Daniel Durham, north by Peter Sallins, east by Francis Brown.

****

Sandiford, John

200 acres, St. John Parish

Granted February 7, 1775   Grant Book M, page 1052

Bounded on the north by James Brown, northwest by Raymond Demere.

****

Saunders, Lydia

550 acres, St. John Parish

Surveyed November 16, 1758   Plat Book C, page 325

Granted May 1, 1759   Grant Book B, page 95

****

Screven, James

100 acres, St. John Parish

Surveyed August 17, 1771 or
        September 12, 1772   Plat Book C, pages 353 and 354

Granted August 4, 1772   Grant Book I, page 709

Bounded on the northeast by Isaac Horshins, northwest by Thomas
Cato.

****

Screven, James

196 acres, St. John Parish

Granted January 3, 1775   Grant Book M, page 940

Bounded on the northwest by William Baker and William Liddle,
southwest by John Eliott, southeast by Quarterman.

****

Sertain, John

100 acres, St. John Parish

Surveyed April 25, 1759   Plat Book C, page 323

Granted December 3, 1760   Grant Book C, page 53

Surveyed as John Sartin and granted as John Sertain.

****

Shave, John

200 acres, District of Midway

Granted May 15, 1756   Grant Book A, page 111

****

Shave, John

150 acres, St. John Parish

Surveyed October 17, 1759   Plat Book C, page 324

Granted July 1, 1760   Grant Book B, page 393

****

Sheaves, Richard

100 acres, St. John Parish

Granted March 2, 1773   Grant Book I, page 921

Bounded on the north by Davis, east by William Swinton, south-west by Thomas Cato.

****

Sheftall, Benjamin

200 acres, St. John Parish

Surveyed May 25, 1757   Plat Book C, page 330

No grant recorded.

Bounded on the east by Daniel Demetry, south and west by salt marsh.

****

Shepherd, Thomas

200 acres, St. John Parish

Surveyed April 17, 1772   Plat Book C, page 349

Granted July 5, 1774   Grant Book M, page 115

Bounded on the south by Dr. Hall.

****

Sheppard, Alexander

150 acres, St. John Parish

Surveyed March 31, 1762   Plat Book C, page 322

Granted November 2, 1762   Grant Book D, page 228

Bounded on the northeast by Benjamin Baker, southeast by John Graves, southwest by William Low.

****

Shruder, Thomas

600 acres, St. John Parish

Granted July 3, 1770   Grant Book I, page 60

Bounded on the north by Canoochee River.

****

Shruder, Thomas

100 acres, St. John Parish

Surveyed May 30, 1770   Plat Book C, page 320

No grant recorded.

Bounded by Thomas Shruder and Canoochee River.

****

Simmons, Elizabeth

500 acres, District of Midway, St. John Parish

Surveyed September 17, 1756   Plat Book C, page 335

Granted October 2, 1759   Grant Book B, page 252

Bounded on the north by Andrew Way.

****

Simpson, John

600 acres, St. John Parish

Surveyed February 2, 1770   Plat Book C, page 345

Granted June 5, 1771   Grant Book I, page 352

Plat says tract located in Sunbury.

****

Simpson, William

300 acres, St. John Parish

Surveyed December 19, 1771   Plat Book C, page 349

Granted June 2, 1772   Grant Book I, page 630

Plat shows tract surrounding David Dix on three sides.

****

Smallwood, Matthew

350 acres, St. John Parish

Surveyed July 12, 1759   Plat Book C, page 300

Granted September 25, 1760   Grant Book B, page 533

Bounded on the north by Robert Smallwood.

****

Smallwood, Matthew

200 acres, St. John Parish

Surveyed January 5, 1762   Plat Book C, page 328

Granted May 1, 1764   Grant Book E, page 6

Bounded on the south by Audley Maxwell, north by said Matthew
Smallwood, west by vacant land. Plat shows tract bounded on the
west by Robert Smallwood.

****

Smallwood, Matthew

100 acres, St. John Parish

Surveyed April 28, 1762   Plat Book C, page 314

Granted March 7, 1769   Grant Book G, page 292

Bounded on the north by said Matthew Smallwood, east by Robert Smallwood, west by John Stevens.

****

Smallwood, Matthew

200 acres, St. John Parish

Surveyed December 9, 1768   Plat Book C, page 312

No grant recorded.

Bounded on the southwest by Robert Smallwood, northeast by Dr. Hall and John Miller.

****

Smallwood, Robert

150 acres, District of Newport

Surveyed September 26, 1755   Plat Book C, page 307

Granted March 5, 1756   Grant Book B, page 10

Tract located one mile west of John Michel, bounded on the west by Mary Bateman, north by John Quarterman, east by Joseph Massey.

****

Smallwood, Robert

200 acres, St. John Parish

Surveyed March 19, 1759   Plat Book C, page 324

Granted August 7, 1759   Grant Book B, page 253

****

Smallwood, Robert

70 acres, St. John Parish

Surveyed March 12, 1761   Plat Book C, pages 320 and 425

Granted October 4, 1763   Grant Book D, page 350

Bounded on the north by said Robert Smallwood.

****

Smallwood, Robert

80 acres, St. John Parish

Surveyed August 30, 1769   Plat Book C, page 334

Granted March 6, 1770   Grant Book H, page 40

Tract adjoins the settlements of said Robert Smallwood being part of a tract of 200 acres heretofore ordered to and surveyed for Matthew Smallwood. Bounded on the southwest and northwest by said Robert Smallwood.

****

Smith, Thomas

150 acres, District of Newport

Granted September 30, 1757   Grant Book A, page 481

Bounded on the northeast by James Mackay.

****

Spencer, John

500 acres, District of Newport

Surveyed October 28, 1756   Plat Book C, page 319

Granted December 9, 1756   Grant Book A, page 375

Bounded on the southwest by John Stevens, southeast by Mary Bateman.

****

Spencer, Richard

500 acres, District of Newport

Granted September 8, 1756   Grant Book A, page 210

****

Stacey, John

100 acres, St. John Parish

Surveyed April 30, 1772   Plat Book C, page 352

Granted August 2, 1774   Grant Book M, page 261

Bounded on the southeast by Benjamin Farley and John Shave, southwest by said John Stacey.

****

Stacey, John

250 acres, St. John Parish

Granted February 7, 1775   Grant Book M, page 1049

Bounded on the north by Thomas Shepherd, south by Benjamin Farley, John Stacey, and John Baker, east by Doctor Hall.

****

Stacy, John

100 acres, St. John Parish

Surveyed March 28, 1771   Plat Book C, page 343

Granted June 5, 1771   Grant Book I, page 350

Bounded on the northeast by John Edwards, southwest by John Baker, southeast by John Shave and the said grantee.

****

Starr, John

200 acres, St. John Parish

Surveyed October 29, 1774   Plat Book C, page 427

No grant recorded.

Bounded on the northwest by James Dukes, southeast by William Deveaux.

****

Stephens, David

500 acres on Midway River

Granted March 5, 1756   Grant Book A, page 104

Tract either in District of Ogeechee or District of Midway. Located at the head of Davis Swamp on the northwest corner of lands alloted to James Donnam, Jr., on the North Branch, Midway River. Bounded on the east by James Donnam.

****

Stephens, Joseph

300 acres, St. John Parish

Granted May 5, 1767   Grant Book F, page 255

Bounded on the north by Samuel Burnley.

****

Stevens, John

500 acres, District of Midway

Surveyed October 1, 1755   Plat Book C, page 333

Granted January 16, 1756   Grant Book A, page 85

Bounded on the east and north by Edward Way.

****

Stevens, John

500 acres, District of Midway

Surveyed October 1, 1755   Plat Book C, page 333

Granted May 15, 1756   Grant Book A, page 177

Bounded on the east by Joseph, Mary, and Sarah Oswald, west by
said John Stevens.

****

Stevens, John

500 acres, District of Midway

Granted May 15, 1756   Grant Book A, page 178

Bounded on the south by said John Stevens.

****

Stevens, John

200 acres, District of Midway

Surveyed May 27, 1755   Plat Book C, page 332

Granted May 15, 1756   Grant Book A, page 179

Bounded on the northeast and southeast by said John Stevens.

****

Stevens, John

233 acres, St. John Parish

Granted May 1, 1759   Grant Book B, page 89

Bounded on the southeast by John Stevens, southwest by said
Stevens.

****

Stevens, John

67½ acres, St. John Parish

Granted May 1, 1759   Grant Book B, page 90

Bounded on the southwest by Sarah Mitchell, northwest by Joseph Gibbons, northeast by William Baker.

****

Stevens, John

100 acres, St. John Parish

Surveyed January 29, 1762 Plat Book C, page 322

Granted April 1, 1764   Grant Book D, page 412

Bounded on the northeast by Joseph Oswald, southeast by said John Stevens, south by John Spencer.

****

Stevens, John

100 acres, St. John Parish

Surveyed April 12, 1770 Plat Book C, page 306

Granted June 5, 1770   Grant Book I, page 33

Bounded on the southwest by Joseph Wright and William Oswell, northeast by Matthew Smallwood, northwest by said John Stevens. Plat shows tract bounded on the southwest by Joseph Way instead of Joseph Wright.

****

Stevens, John

100 acres, St. John Parish

Granted November 1, 1774 Grant Book M, page 736

Bounded on the north by John Mitchell, west by vacant land, all other sides by said John Stevens.

****

Stevens, John

200 acres, St. John Parish

Surveyed October 11, 1759   Plat Book C, page 427

No grant recorded.

Bounded on the west by Newport River and John Jones, north by
Herriott Crooks, south by John Barnaby.

****

Stevens, John; Osgood, John; Elliott, John; Baker, William;
Bacon, Joseph; Way, Parmenus; Quarterman, John; Winn, John;
Graves, John; Baker, Richard (all trustees)

300 acres, District of Midway

Granted September 8, 1756   Grant Book A, page 327

Bounded on the west by Nathaniel Way. Land granted in trust
for the use of the minister for the time being of the Dissenting
or Congregational Church erected or to be erected in the District
of Midway and Newport.

****

Stevens, Joseph

150 acres, St. John Parish

Surveyed June 11, 1767   Plat Book C, page 315

Granted November 3, 1767   Grant Book F, page 412

Bounded on the northeast by John Stevens, west by said Joseph
Stevens, south by Samuel Burley.

****

Stevens, Samuel

142 acres, St. John Parish

Surveyed July 2, 1768   Plat Book C, page 299

Granted November 1, 1768   Grant Book G, page 221

Bounded on the east by Glebe land, north by John Golding, west
by said Samuel Stevens and Kenneth Baillie, south by Green.

****

Stewart, James

400 acres, St. John Parish

Surveyed September 15, 1769   Plat Book C, page 304

Granted July 4, 1769   Grant Book G, page 369

Bounded on the south by said James Stewart, north by Thomas
Ways, west by Richard Gerardeous and vacant land.

****

Stewart, John

300 acres, St. John Parish

Granted July 1, 1760   Grant Book B, page 421

Bounded on the east by said John Stewart and Joseph Gibbons,
south by William Baker, northwest by David Tobear.

****

Stewart, John

178 acres, St. John Parish

Surveyed December 3, 1761   Plat Book C, page 426

Granted September 7, 1762   Grant Book D, page 192

Bounded on the north by Robert Smallwood and Joseph McKay,
east by Tubear, south and southwest by William Baker and Joseph Way.

****

Stewart, John Jr.

500 acres on South Branch, Newport River

Surveyed December 31, 1755   Plat Book C, page 302

Granted March 5, 1756   Grant Book A, page 77

Bounded on the east by William Graves, west by Benjamin Andrews.

****

Stewart, John Sr.

500 acres, District of Newport

Granted February 7, 1758   Grant Book A, page 637

Bounded on the west by Captain James Mackay.

****

Stiles, Benjamin and Stiles, Samuel

1000 acres, St. John Parish

Surveyed November 19, 1769   Plat Book C, page 318

No grant recorded.

Bounded on the northeast by William Wylly.

****

Stiles, Samuel and Stiles, Benjamin

1000 acres, St. John Parish

Surveyed November 19, 1769   Plat Book C, page 318

No grant recorded.

Bounded on the northeast by William Wylly.

****

Stuart, James

200 acres, St. John Parish

Granted November 1, 1774   Grant Book M, page 730

Bounded on the southwest by Thomas Carter, north by John Jones.

****

Stuart, James

300 acres, St. John Parish

Granted February 7, 1775   Grant Book M, page 1051

Bounded on the southeast by Thomas Shruder and vacant land.

****

Sumners, Edward

500 acres, District of Midway

Granted December 9, 1756   Grant Book A, page 273

Bounded on the east by Benjamin Baker, north by Andrew Collins and John Elliott.

****

Swinton, William

200 acres, St. John Parish

Surveyed June 12, 1760   Plat Book C, pages 326 and 427

Granted April 5, 1763   Grant Book D, page 297

Bounded on the southwest by Josiah Powell and William Baker, east by Kenneth Bailey.

****

Swinton, William

800 acres, St. John Parish

Surveyed July 24, 1764   Plat Book C, page 302

Granted October 31, 1765   Grant Book E, page 320

Bounded on the south by John Quarterman, east by Parmenas Way and William McPherson, north by David Stephen, Maurice Dullia, and Grey Elliott, west by William Baker, Jr.

****

Tannatt, Edmund

500 acres, District of Newport

Surveyed November 14, 1755   Plat Book C, page 363

Granted September 8, 1756   Grant Book A, page 233

Bounded on the east by Thomas and William Carr, northwest by Josiah Osgood and Joseph Winn, southwest by William Peacock, southeast by Captain James Reid.

****

Tannatt, Edmund

500 acres between Midway and Newport Rivers

Granted September 8, 1756   Grant Book A, page 234

Tract was known as Greenwich and located on a southern branch of Newport River. Bounded on the southeast by Newport River, southwest by William Baillou and Richard Hazard.

****

Taylor, James

150 acres, St. John Parish

Surveyed April 30, 1761   Plat Book C, pages 362 and 426

Granted November 2, 1762   Grant Book D, page 238

Bounded on the south by Sylvanus Robinson.

****

Taylor, James

200 acres, St. John Parish

Surveyed July 25, 1769   Plat Book C, page 372

Granted February 6, 1770   Grant Book G, page 530

Bounded on the northwest by said James Taylor.

****

Taylor, Nathan

500 acres, District of Midway

Granted September 30, 1757   Grant Book A, page 438

Bounded on the south by Audley Maxwell, north by William Gore, east by Isaac Lines, west by marshes of Midway River.

****

Telfair, Edward; Cowper, Basil; Telfair, William

1000 acres, St. John Parish

Granted June 5, 1770   Grant Book I, page 42

Bounded partly on the northeast by Henry Lewis Bourguin and partly by vacant land, southwest partly by John Collin and partly by land heretofore laid out, on all other sides by vacant land.

****

Telfair, William; Cowper, Basil; Telfair, Edward

1000 acres, St. John Parish

Granted June 5, 1770   Grant Book I, page 42

Bounded partly on the northeast by Henry Lewis Bourguin and partly by vacant land, southwest partly by John Collin and partly by land heretofore laid out, on all other sides by vacant land.

****

Timmons, John

200 acres, St. John Parish

· Granted November 1, 1774   Grant Book M, page 743

Bounded on the northwest by Butler.

                              ****

Timmons, John

200 acres, St. John Parish

Granted November 1, 1774   Grant Book M, page 744

Bounded on the southeast by Richard Baker and Strong Ashmore.

                              ****

Tobear, David

200 acres, St. John Parish

Surveyed May 17, 1758   Plat Book C, page 364

Granted September 5, 1758   Grant Book B, page 33

Bounded on the north by Joseph Massey.

                              ****

Todd, John Jr.

100 acres, District of Newport

Granted June 7, 1757   Grant Book A, page 414

Bounded on the west by John Todd, Sr., north by South Branch,
Newport River.

                              ****

Todd, John Sr.

100 acres, District of Newport

Granted September 30, 1757   Grant Book A, page 624

Bounded on the north by Newport River, east by John Todd, Jr.

****

Tripp, Isaac

100 acres, District of Newport

Surveyed February 19, 1757   Plat Book C, page 365

Granted December 6, 1757   Grant Book A, page 613

Bounded on the northeast by Lachlan McIntosh,

****

Watson, Nathaniel

100 acres, District of Midway

Granted January 16, 1756   Grant Book A, page 131

Tract located on north side of Midway River (and thus probably
became St. Philip Parish in 1758). Bounded on the west by Collins
Creek, north by John Benett,

****

Way, Andrew

500 acres, District of Newport

Granted December 9, 1756   Grant Book A, page 334

Bounded on the east by John Elliott, west by Isaac Girardeau,
north and south by vacant lands,

****

Way, Andrew

150 acres, St. John Parish

Granted April 13, 1761   Grant Book C, page 158

Bounded on the south by said Andrew Way, north by James Pritchard.

****

Way, Edward

500 acres, District of Midway

Granted January 16, 1756   Grant Book B, page 11

Bounded on the north by John Elliott, west by John Lupton and John Stevens, south by William Baker, east by Edward Sumner.

****

Way, Edward

450 acres, District of Newport

Surveyed May 31, 1757   Plat Book C, page 442

Granted September 30, 1757   Grant Book A, page 540

Bounded on the east by William Dunham, west by John Stewart, Sr. Surveyed as being in District of Midway.

****

Way, Edward

100 acres, St. John Parish

Granted February 3, 1767   Grant Book F, page 81

Bounded on the northeast by Elizabeth Summers, southeast by said Edward Way.

****

Way, Edward

250 acres, District of Newport

Surveyed April 16, 1755   Plat Book C, page 441

Bounded on the west by J. Quarterman.

****

Way, Joseph

500 acres on North Branch, Midway River

Granted March 5, 1756   Grant Book A, page 112

Bounded on the southeast by William Baker, northwest by Joseph Oswald. Tract located either in St. John Parish or St. Philip Parish.

****

Way, Joseph

200 acres, St. John and St. Andrew Parishes

Granted July 5, 1774   Grant Book M, page 141

Bounded on the west by Jacob Lewis, south by Samuel Hasting's estate and vacant land, east by William Dunham's estate and vacant land, north by Joseph Way.

****

Way, Moses

200 acres, District of Newport

Granted September 8, 1756   Grant Book A, page 213

Bounded on the north by Elizabeth Baker.

****

Way, Nathaniel

500 acres, District of Midway

Granted September 8, 1756   Grant Book A, page 327

****

Way, Parmenus

500 acres, District of Midway

Granted October 1, 1755   Grant Book A, page 83

Bounded on the east by marshes of Midway River, west by Nathan Taylor.

****

Way, Parmenus

300 acres, District of Midway

Granted September 8, 1756   Grant Book A, page 326

Bounded on the west by John Davis and John Durham, southeast by John Maxwell.

****

Way, Parmenus

100 acres, St. John Parish

Granted July 1, 1760   Grant Book B, page 473

Bounded on the west by said Way, south by Taylor and Quarterman.

****

Way, Parmenus; Osgood, John; Stevens, John; Elliott, John;
Baker, William; Bacon, Joseph; Quarterman, John; Winn, John;
Graves, John; Baker, Richard (all trustees)

300 acres, District of Midway

Granted September 8, 1756   Grant Book A, page 327

Bounded on the west by Nathaniel Way. Land granted in trust
for the use of the minister for the time being of the Dissenting
or Congregational Church erected or to be erected in the District
of Midway and Newport.

****

Way, Samuel

500 acres, District of Midway

Granted May 15, 1756   Grant Book A, page 203

Bounded on the south by John Mitchell.

****

Way, Thomas

200 acres, District of Newport

Granted September 30, 1757   Grant Book B, page 16

****

Way, Thomas

100 acres, St. John Parish

Surveyed August 15, 1759   Plat Book C, page 431

No grant recorded.

Bounded on the northeast by William Quarterman, south by Elisha
Butler and Thomas Way.

****

Way, William

200 acres, St. John Parish

Granted August 1, 1769   Grant Book G, page 400

****

Way, William

300 acres, St. John Parish

Granted January 3, 1775   Grant Book M, page 967

Bounded on the north by William Way.

****

West, Charles

400 acres, District of Newport

Granted January 16, 1756   Grant Book A, page 99

Bounded on the west by Moses Way.

****

West, Charles

300 acres, District of Newport

Granted June 7, 1757   Grant Book A, page 385

Bounded on the north by Alexander Ross.

****

West, Charles

400 acres, St. John Parish

Granted December 3, 1760   Grant Book C, page 3

Bounded on the north by said Charles West.

****

West, Charles

100 acres, St. John Parish

Granted December 3, 1760   Grant Book C, page 5

Bounded on the southeast by said Charles West.

****

West, Charles

291 acres, St. John Parish

Granted April 13, 1761   Grant Book C, page 7

Bounded on the east by Latimore, southeast by marsh of South Newport River, west by said Charles West and Alexander Ross.

****

West, Charles

200 acres, St. John Parish

Granted February 5, 1765   Grant Book E, page 103

Bounded on the southwest by said Charles West and vacant land, north by Moses Way and Joseph Goodbee, south by Stephen Williams.

****

White, Thomas

100 acres, District of Newport

Granted December 6, 1757   Grant Book B, page 365

Bounded on the southeast and southwest by Newport River and the Bain Creek.

****

Williams, Abraham

133 acres, St. John Parish

Granted January 3, 1764   Grant Book D, page 372

Bounded on the west by John Burnet, north by Josiah Phrisby and vacant marsh, east by Thomas Clancy, south and southeast by vacant marsh and North Newport River.

****

Williams, Stephen

300 acres, St. John Parish

Granted May 1, 1759   Grant Book B, page 163

****

Wilson, William

100 acres, St. John Parish

Surveyed July 13, 1759   Plat Book C, page 430

Granted February 5, 1760   Grant Book B, page 447

Bounded on the south by Benjamin Andrew, west by John Cain and John Humphrys.

****

Winn, John

500 acres, District of Midway

Granted May 14, 1756   Grant Book A, page 109

Bounded on the east and southeast by Thomas Carr and Edmund Tanet, west and southwest by Rebeckah Quarterman and Joseph Winn, northwest by John Osgood, clerk.

****

Winn, John

500 acres, District of Midway

Granted May 15, 1756   Grant Book A, page 110

Bounded on the southwest by Moses Way and Charles West, north
by Richard and Elizabeth Baker, east by Benjamin Andrew.

****

Winn, John

350 acres, St. John Parish

Granted May 1, 1759   Grant Book B, page 433

Bounded on the south by Mark Carr, southwest by said Winn and
John Osgood, north by Edward Summers and Benjamin Baker, east
by Samuel Bacon.

****

Winn, John

600 acres, St. John Parish

Granted July 4, 1769   Grant Book G, page 375

Bounded on the northwest by Lydia Sanders, north by Audley
Maxwell and John Davis, south by Benjamin Andrew.

****

Winn, John; Osgood, John; Stevens, John; Elliott, John; Baker,
William; Bacon, Joseph; Way, Parmenus; Quarterman, John; Graves,
John; Baker, Richard (all trustees)

300 acres, District of Midway

Granted September 8, 1756   Grant Book A, page 327

Bounded on the west by Nathaniel Way. Land granted in trust
for the use of the minister for the time being of the Dissenting
or Congregational Church erected or to be erected in the District
of Midway and Newport.

****

Winn, Joseph

200 acres, District of Newport

Granted December 6, 1757   Grant Book A, page 499

Tract located at the head of Newport River. Bounded on the north by Josiah Osgood, northwest by Edmund Tannatt, west by John Winn, southeast by Rebecka Quarterman.

****

Wright, James

1400 acres, St. John Parish

Granted September 5, 1769   Grant Book G, page 416

Bounded on the east by said James Wright.

****

Wright, James

600 acres, St. John Parish

Granted September 5, 1769   Grant Book G, page 417

Bounded on the southwest by said James Wright.

****

Wright, James

1000 acres, St. John Parish

Granted March 6, 1770   Grant Book G, page 566

Bounded on the southwest by said James Wright.

****

Wright, James

1000 acres, St. John Parish

Granted March 6, 1770   Grant Book G, page 567

Bounded on the southeast by James Graham and vacant land, northwest by said James Wright and vacant land.

****

Wylly, William

800 acres, St. John Parish

Granted September 5, 1769   Grant Book G, page 419

Bounded on the northwest by William Deveaux.

****

Yonge, Henry

300 acres, District of Midway

Granted April 5, 1757   Grant Book A, page 360

Bounded on the northeast by marshes of Midway River, east by Lewis Johnson, west by Henry Hamilton.

****

Young, Thomas

300 acres, St. John Parish

Granted January 6, 1767   Grant Book F, page 45

Bounded on the north by Adam Bosomworth, west by Clement Martin, south partly by John Sandiford and partly by vacant land.

****

Young, Thomas

57 acres, St. John Parish

Granted July 5, 1774   Grant Book H, page 109

Bounded on the south by Thomas White, on all other sides by said grantee.

****

Young, Thomas

90 acres, St. John Parish

Granted July 5, 1774   Grant Book H, page 108

Bounded on the east by North Newport River, north by John Burnet and Joseph White, south by Boin Creek and John Lynn, west by said John Lynn now lands belonging to said grantee.

****

Young, Thomas

100 acres, Bermuda Island, St. John Parish

Granted November 1, 1774   Grant Book M, page 768

Tract is surplus land granted John Jones, deceased, for 350 acres on Bermuda Island, now the property of said Thomas Young.

****

Young, Thomas

141 acres, St. John Parish

Granted November 1, 1774   Grant Book M, page 769

Bounded on the west by Raymound Demere, north by said Thomas Young, south by Francis Brown.

****

Young, Thomas

311½ acres, St. John Parish

Granted December 6, 1774   Grant Book M, page 837

****

www.ingramcontent.com/pod-product-compliance
Lightning Source LLC
Chambersburg PA
CBHW080617270326
41928CB00016B/3103